IN LEAGUE
WITH THE STONES

IN LEAGUE
WITH THE STONES

One Woman's Journey of Faith

by
Patricia Kennedy Helman

THE BRETHREN PRESS, ELGIN, ILL

"The Prayer of Faith," by Hannah More Kohaus, quoted on page 59, is used by permission of *Unity,* Unity Village, Missouri.

Library of Congress Cataloging in Publication Data

Helman, Patricia Kennedy.
    In league with the stones.

    1.   Helman, Patricia Kennedy.   I.   Title.
BX7843.H44A34   248'.2'0924   [B]   76-13639
ISBN 0-87178-416-5

To my Mother and Father

for the gifts

of life and love

AN INTRODUCTORY NOTE
by
ANNA B. MOW

Several years ago I was invited to help in a family camp in Kansas. I must confess that I accepted the invitation mainly because I wanted to see what kind of a wife Blair Helman had chosen.

When I learned to know Pat I was delighted. Every contact through the years since has increased my appreciation of her.

She is an artist of true spiritual quality. She thinks like the psalmists of old; all nature speaks to her of God. Whether it is in the turn of a phrase, or in the beautiful Christmas angels she fashions, God's creativeness works through her. As wife, mother, hostess, or friend she helps one see better the quality of God's love.

Pat is indeed *Free to Be a Woman* (the title of her first book), and in *In League With the Stones* we find out the kind of a delightful woman she is.

CONTENTS

"Behold, happy is the man whom
  God reproves;
therefore despise not the chastening
  of the Almighty.
For he wounds, but he binds up;
  he smites, but his hands heal.
He will deliver you from six
  troubles;
in seven there shall be no evil touch
  you.
In famine he will redeem you from
  death,
and in war from the power of the
  sword.
You shall be hid from the scourge
  of the tongue,
and shall not fear destruction
  when it comes.
At destruction and famine you shall
  laugh,
and shall not fear the beasts of
  the earth;
for you shall be *in league with the
  stones* of the field,
and the beasts of the field shall
  be at peace with you."

Job. 5:17-23

PROLOGUE

If, as we are told in Ecclesiastes, there is a time for everything, I wonder if there is a time for unmasking, for openness, for a sharing of self that is both satisfying and yet somewhat terrifying. For, with too much openness, one becomes vulnerable to others. When the mask comes off you may expose strength; but alas, the weakness is there for everyone to see; and often such weakness calls forth responses that hurt and puzzle one who has been so indiscreet as to try to be authentic.

At that incalculable risk I edge the mask off slowly and hesitatingly, recalling a time many springs ago when events occurred within our family that were destined to change us all. They were not cataclysmic, earthshaking events wherein the sky falls and the earth cleaves and destruction is rampant. They were more like little tremors where you think you felt the house shake from more than a passing wind—where the pictures have become crooked on the wall, and things in general seem slightly awry.

It was a spring crammed with activity, with rigorous schedules from early morning until late at night. There was the tension of constant meetings of planes and trains, of saying rushed hellos and good-byes, of two adults facing innumerable audiences and of two little people waiting in a home embroiled in the hectic activities that accelerate in a college community in the springtime.

I see the big man writing speeches in the early hours of the morning, his face haggard and gray, his eyes lusterless. I see him driving over miles of traffic-laden highways, frantically pushing ahead. He passes one truck, a car, a semi-trailer. He glances at his watch—almost time to speak—hurry—hurry. His foot is heavy on the gas pedal. Now for directions to the school. He sees the big yellow brick building that looks like a thousand other American schools.

The seniors are outside, talking in small groups, laughing, admiring each other in their caps and gowns. The big man is out of the car—they spot him, the commencement speaker, the last hurdle between them and graduation.

The big man turns into his driveway. The light is on—she is up—he must tell her not to wait up for him now—she needs her rest. There are so many things he must tell her—how much he loves her, how the sight of this house with the light burning for him makes it all seem worth it—he'll tell her when he isn't so tired.

He goes into the house and she is waiting for him, having fallen asleep in a chair. He wakens her—

"Come on. Let's go upstairs."

"Oh, hi. How did the speech go?"

He mumbles a response—too tired to talk. There is so much they should say to each other, but weariness cancels communication. "Goodnight." "Goodnight."

The woman has her own involvements. I see her in a flurry of housecleaning and sense the futile frustration of never quite getting finished with the job at hand. She is many things: scrubwoman, speechmaker, laundress, hostess, chauffeur, mother, campus first lady. She moves with haste and tension—changing clothes to suit her many roles.

She doesn't feel well. She takes many pills, and scrutinizes her face in the mirror for pallor and deep circles under her eyes, which will reveal too much. She is very tired—movement becomes effort, but she moves continually.

I see the small family with barely time to rejoice together over the news that in November a newcomer will come into their lives. Maybe he—of course, this time it will be a boy—maybe he will change their lives. Yes, that is the answer. He will bring them together again in that charmed circle of warmth and love that used to be.

They will find a cradle—there's a lovely Jenny Lind cradle in that quaint little shop on Highway 13. They will gather around the cradle and look into his little face, and love will flow through them and around them, and they will wonder how they let themselves get caught up in this hectic life. Apart when they could be together—away when they could be home—busy with the periphery of life when they could center down their lives. Yes—November will make the difference. They've waited for him so long.

I see the family anxious and waiting. The doctor comes once, twice, three times. Frantic telephone calls are made. Yes, Mrs. Brown will see to the kitchen for the reception for the seniors. Yes, Evelyn will take care of the punch table—don't worry—rest—so you can be on your feet when the two hundred seniors arrive.

The pain becomes unbearable. The big man is awake with her through the long night. The doctor must be called. "I hate to waken him."

The two little girls are awakened. They want to talk to her, but speech is too difficult through pain and weakness. She has a strange pallor that looks almost green beneath the shaded lights. They hover over her. They don't want to cry, but her eyes are far away from them, and this isn't the mother with the happy, laughing face they know. The big man pushes them gently from the room. "She'll be all right." Reassure them. But who will reassure him?

Another telephone call to a neighbor. "Of course, they can come and sleep here. What else can we do— we're so sorry."

The ambulance slithers silently to the door. A grayness engulfs her as she leaves the house on a stretcher. So he will not be with them in November after all.

The hospital is a dream world—figures move silently—mouths move but no sound is heard. Or strange sounds are everywhere—someone is slapping babies—so many babies in such a small hospital. "No, dear, it's only typewriter keys you hear." Why are they shoveling corn in the hospital? "You are silly—no one is shoveling corn." "I hear them; I hear them!" "Oh, the girl is scooping up cracked ice from the dispenser—rest, now rest." There's a hissing noise— it's constant! "Only the drinking fountain—rest, rest!"

The big man comes through the door, observes the "No Visitors" sign with satisfaction. He can only stay a few minutes—they miss her—they need her. He'll make it through the week—four commencement speeches; miles of driving; his baccalaureate address, the capstone of the college year; many hands to shake; many banquets to attend; many speeches of a few well-chosen words. But it will end. When it's all over we'll bring you home. Now you must rest.

The little family I have described is my family. The big man is Blair, born on Christmas Day in 1920. Blair's young mother was involved in the death struggle trying to give birth to her firstborn. His father, in an humble and prayerful way, promised God that if the child could be saved, he would guide him into a life of service. Blair and his mother were spared, and his early life was lived under the shadow of a promise that gave shape and purpose to his destiny.

From the humblest of beginnings, his dreams included a goal that involved Christian service and education. Armed with a deep faith, keen intelligence, and an intense drive, he made a startling metamorphosis from a coal miner to a college president in fifteen years. His unusually broad shoulders are reminders of the years in the mines; and his rugged, pensive countenance gives a suggestion of one who understands the interior way of life.

In that spring of long ago the little people were not really little anymore. Bunny was thirteen, a Dresden blonde with the fairest of fair skin, hair that turns gold when the least light is cast upon it, and eyes that are a lovely and beguiling blue.

She gives credence to the rhyme "But a child that is born on the Sabbath Day is good, and wise, and happy, and gay." And this particular Sabbath Day was Easter; and while the world rejoiced over the new birth of the Risen Lord, Blair and I held Bunny in our arms, a beautiful symbol of new life, and hope, and eternity.

Dawn was almost ready to turn nine. She came to us in that fleeting moment when the night shades pull away from the heavens to reveal the pearly pink dawning of an August morning. She was truly a child of the morning—eager, alive, intense—always ready to turn the most prosaic plans into high adventure. Dawn typified the true American brownette: brown hair, highlighted with gold at her hair line and across her brows, and a deep-toned skin that turns berry-brown in the summer. Her eyes are a mellow brown, and constantly reveal her temperament to the world. Sparkling and dancing with delight, somber with compassion, stormy and defiant when her world is amiss.

The lady was myself, Patricia called Pat, an ambivalent, trying to be all things to all people. And it is I who will risk removing the mask. I will try to tell you how I feel about my life and my faith—what things and places and persons have fueled the engine that moves me to accept specific values and respond to life in a particular way.

I begin that process by affirming that I have always had an awareness of being surrounded and uplifted by love. My parents were warm and openly affectionate, and there was never any doubt that literally and figuratively their arms were open, ready to receive their children in love. To this day, when I return to my family home, my own worries and concerns fall away. I feel childlike again as the love of my parents settles around me with a security and steadfastness that nothing can replace. My family circle also included two older sisters and a younger brother.

In this day when a book like Bach and Wyden's *The Intimate Enemy* makes its impact, and calls for openness in negative as well as positive ways, I can only say that this is no new idea to the Kennedy family in which I grew up. Our parents—unwittingly, I think—gave us the gift of honest emotions. We learned to be fearful neither of engaging in conflict nor of dispensing love.

THE LODESTAR

Throughout that frantic spring of 1961, we must have typified the American family. If the articles in newspapers and magazines do not give the lie to the culture in which we find ourselves, then we were shining examples. We were too heavily scheduled, we had allowed too many demands to encroach upon our time, we could not spend needful time with the girls, and communication between Blair and me reached a low point in our married lives. Not because of any overt conflict, but because our comings and goings were not synchronized, and barriers of time and geographical distance became insurmountable.

In the midst of this cultured holocaust there was a lodestar. It shone above us, and our hungry hearts and wistful eyes fastened to it as the one steadying and directing thought that controlled us and kept us from flying completely apart.

During fourteen years of married life, Blair and I had never had a vacation. True, we had traveled many miles together. We were well acquainted with major highways in America. Our daughters, Bunny and Dawn, had seen more of their native land by the time they were ten than Blair and I had seen in all of our "growing up" lives.

But always on such trips, ulterior motives were present. Our church's Annual Conference had taken us to the east coast and west, and to the south and north. But being involved in leadership roles in a conference of seven thousand people is no vacation.

Our home in Indiana is the dividing point between our two family homes in Iowa and Pennsylvania. Many trips have been made over the Turnpike to Grandmother's house; but visiting relatives, no matter how beloved, is not a vacation either.

For me a true vacation means "vacating" oneself from ordinary pursuits and from normal personal contacts. It means being away and alone as a family, and it means time spent, not in battling traffic, but reading, resting, and doing those things which you find satisfyingly fun. I think this is especially important if your life is public by the nature of your vocation. Many persons find themselves so geared to satisfying the demands of others, whether consciously or otherwise, that time alone becomes an essential ingredient for their physical, mental, and spiritual well-being.

The specific motivation for our vacation was, as usual, not just for the fun of it: Blair had some important writing to get done. This project had cast its perpetual shadow over him during the five years we had been at Manchester College. It was apparent, shortly after we arrived, that his job would allow no leisure time to finish the necessary writing. If time was ever available, it was only in short periods. Occasionally he tried leaving us. He went out of the state and literally holed up in a hotel. But Blair is basically a family man, and the frustrations of self-imposed loneliness and homesickness invaded his privacy and cut into the efficiency with which he ordinarily wrote.

In desperation he decided the solution would be to rent a cottage during the month of July, take us along, and write. He had visions of getting far away, of isolating himself and his thoughts from all the possible intrusions with which his life was fraught.

And so the search began for the right place. But one of the great paradoxes of America's vacationlands is that you are hard put to find anything that is isolated. The joys to be found in a cottage on the lake are for sale, and many people are in the market to buy joy.

When it seemed our efforts to find the right spot were going to be fruitless, our dear friends Hubert and Alice Newcomer began to give us glowing reports of the vacation they had spent the previous summer at Point Betsie. As they spoke of the broad sweep of Lake Michigan, the miles of isolated beach, the peaceful background of the dunes, the drama of the Coast Guard lighthouse, we knew our search was ended. One word of warning they gave us—the beach was sandy but also stony—hordes of stones were tossed onto the beach by the waves, fossilized corals from another era. The thought of finding these fossil treasures only whetted our desires to go there.

After some frantic correspondence with Arvid Zetterberg, owner and keeper of the sandy domain, and much conjecturing about whether or not we would be able to pay the price, the decision was made. And the cottage at Point Betsie literally became the lodestar that gave purpose to the spring.

At the end of those hectic days when it seemed we

were drained of our very selves, Blair or I would remind each other that July would arrive on schedule and Point Betsie would be a reality. Often in the midst of a wistful good-bye, as we left Bunny and Dawn for a long evening away, or perhaps a weekend, they would console each other with the fact that we had actually rented a cottage and that the four of us would be together for a whole month. "Just us! Just us!" Dawn would say happily, and the vision of Point Betsie which she fashioned with her child's soul was graphic.

I hugged the thought to me constantly that there was to be a time and place where Blair and I could restock our minds and our souls. For fourteen years, as a minister and teacher, and finally as a college president, Blair had been giving of himself. And a wife has to give, too. We were tired, with a tiredness that sleep could not cure—a tiredness that ached for the peacefulness of a silent summer afternoon and the whispered lullaby of the dunes.

One night when Blair had come home from a long trip, he settled wearily in his chair and said, "You know what I wish. I wish I felt the same kind of tiredness I felt when I was mining coal. After I dug coal all day, my muscles ached, my back felt stretched out of shape, but I'd walk three miles home, fall into bed, and die until morning. When I got up, my arms were okay, my back felt normal, and I felt like digging coal again. Now when I get up, I don't feel much different than when I went to bed." And thus it is that the weariness of the mind and spirit manifests itself. So Point Betsie became our panacea—our cure-all for tired bodies and spirits.

As spring dragged on, my physical condition

24

became consistently worse. When the dreaded mis-carriage occurred, I was thrown into mental and physical despair. During those days at the hospital, overcome by the complete weariness and weakness that follow a shocking loss of blood, Point Betsie again became a sustaining thought. In the midst of pain, accompanied by an overwhelming sense of loss, my tired mind dwelt on Point Betsie—how it must look—how it must be—what it would mean to us as a family, and what it would mean to each of us as individuals. Now it was obvious that the experience was not to be only of therapeutic value for our spirits but would literally be a time of physical recuperation.

As I lay in the hospital, I thought of the silence, the water, the wind, and the sun as healing agents—healing soul and body and giving all of us a sense of newness of life. And lying there, I was impressed with that sense of the sovereignty of God in my life. In that sense I was in league with the stones, a part of the wholeness and unity of God's creation. I was one of those to whom Teilhard de Chardin dedicated *The Divine Milieu*, "For those who love the world."

What my soul cried for most was just time to think. I remember as a child how I loved to find a solitary spot—sometimes in an accessible tree—sometimes in the swing at the grape arbor—and sometimes just to sit on the curbstone and let my thoughts wander at random.

I could not remember when the luxury of an un-cluttered afternoon had been mine. I could not recall having had time to nestle against the warm earth and lazily look skyward and let my spirit freely say, "O God, what is man (woman) that thou art mindful of him (her)? Who am I? What do you want me to do? Why can't I be better? Why is pain and separation a necessary part of life?"

I looked forward to the isolation that Point Betsie would provide as an opportunity to think about the absolutes in my own life. I wanted to give Bunny and Dawn a legacy—not in cash or property, but I wanted them to know how their mother felt about life and its meaning, about God and our relationship to him, about the people we love, about the people we relate to only in quick, sporadic ways.

I have several friends, sainted souls, who are friends through the written word only. Reading the insightful writings of numerous great Christians and wedding their ideas to my own knowledge and faith leads me to certain conclusions.

Forbes Robinson wrote in a little pamphlet published by Pendle Hill and called *An Inward Legacy:* "The only reality underlying and explaining our existence must be personal. I know I am a person, and that everything that has affected me or moved me or has changed my life has come from other persons. If this is the absolute or reality by which I live, then the key thing in my life will be my relationship as a personal being to other personal beings."

He goes on to say that having been nurtured in the framework of a Christian society and having been moved by the Christian experience, he believes that the ultimate in reality comes when the spirit of Christ invades a personality and a life is lived through his unsurpassed love for all personality and all life.

I accept unqualifiedly this insight from Forbes Robinson. The acceptance of it reminds me that God's name is Love and that I am called to live out that supra-personal value that Christ personalized for us. And I must personalize it too, must put it to work in my own life. So it was that I held these thoughts as we were drawn closer and closer by the magnetic force of the lodestar that brightened the darkness of that hectic spring, a sandy paradise called Point Betsie.

FIRST IMPRESSIONS

Our anticipation, which had built up to a sort of contained hysteria, gave way to unrestrained joy when we came upon an obscure sign on M-22, the weathered message being: Point Betsie; U. S. Coast Guard Station, 1 mile; Lake Michigan, 1 mile.

We turned onto the county road that wound languidly around the dunes. When the red roof of the lighthouse became visible, the girls squealed with delight. In a moment we were confronted with the majesty of the lake, the road coming to an abrupt end only a few feet from the water's edge.

As we turned left from the road, our Cape Cod cottage came into view. It sat upon a knoll commanding a full view of the lake. The white shingles were clean and trim, and the bright blue shutters made the house seem even whiter.

As soon as the car stopped, Dawn and Bunny deserted us for a whirlwind examination of the cottage. They ran from room to room, exclaiming over major and minor discoveries. They hurried up to the dormer that went completely across the cottage to find the maid's room of which we had had such glowing reports. Bunny had elected to isolate herself in the maid's room, evidently envisioning some huge and private paradise. When she came downstairs her face was crestfallen, and she announced in a disillusioned voice that she guessed she wouldn't sleep in the maid's room after all. And so she learned a reality of life. The servants do not have the choice rooms in the household.

The rooms of the cottage were large and plentiful, the kitchen well stocked with most of the utensils and equipment a family would find needful.

A mosaic fireplace dominated the living room. It was constructed of huge stones that had once been part of the treasure trove of Lake Michigan. Later, when we learned to know and love Arvid and Winifred Zetterberg, from whom we rented the cottage, the fireplace took on more meaning. As we learned to know more about their life together, which was an exemplary course in how married people should relate to one another, we grew acquainted with their joys and disappointments. The stones in the great mosaic fireplace had been carried up from the lake by Winifred and her sons Stephen and Pierre. After Pierre's tragic death in 1945 in World War II at the Battle of the Bulge, the fireplace suddenly took on a spiritual dimension for a part of Pierre had found its way into this central focus of light and warmth in the Cape Cod cottage.

On the mantle was a model of an old sailing ship, the sails awry and the metal tarnished. Even in this battered condition it added flavor to the room, and the warmth of knotty pine walls and the nautical lamps and fixtures gave one the intimate feeling of having just entered the captain's cabin.

Beside the ship's model lay a large pair of field glasses. Dawn pounced on them and darted for the front door. She stood on the cottage walk, the ties of her red straw hat waving wildly, her blue jacket billowing from the strong winds. Lifting the glasses to her eyes, she looked towards the lake and shouted, "I'm Christopher Columbus, and I see land." We all agreed that even Columbus would have enjoyed the caricature she made. He discovered the New World, but with no more exhilaration than Dawn was discovering Point Betsie.

Across the front of the cottage was a large sun porch, the huge glass windows presenting an unending expanse of the lake. At one end of the porch a tiny dining room was enclosed. It was just large enough for the four of us, and the girls were enchanted with the coziness it offered. From the dining room windows, which faced north and west, one could see both the lighthouse and the lake. It was decided at once that we would have to rotate places at the table so we could have equal time at dining with the view.

Blair took one of the bedrooms for his study, and from the time we arrived, this room was off limits to the rest of us. Only a real emergency, like finding an extra-special treasure on the beach or announcing a coffee break, would allow the three females a knock on the door.

We soon decided that our cottage was the "dooriest" house we had ever been in. Each of the three downstairs bedrooms had private exits to the outdoors. This encouraged early morning hikes over the dunes, or a frigid dip in the lake without creating a general disturbance. The big bathroom had its own exit also, so no one had any excuse to prance through the house dripping glacial waters. All in all, there were

31

seven entrances from outdoors to the first floor. Early in our stay there we tried to lock up at night, but it was so involved that we gave up and took our chances with the rest of the sparse population.

In a matter of eight or ten steps from one of the several back doors, our backyard stopped being a normal yard, and turned into a wonderful sand dune. It looked like a great round bowl of brown sugar, the center of which had been eaten away. It was a most inviting sand dune—we couldn't just look—we had to jump in and delight in the smooth warmness of the sand.

"This is the biggest sandpile I've ever had!" said Dawn, between much jumping and panting. The backyard was only one of the many surprises in store for us.

Blair and I left the girls still reveling in the sand, and went to the front of the house to take stock of our surroundings. To the right of us was a smaller cottage, unoccupied at the time. And right on the edge of the lake, just a stone's throw in a northwesterly direction, the Coast Guard house dominated the view. At one time this had housed a company of coastguardsmen, enough sailors to man emergency boats needed when Lake Michigan went on one of its legendary rampages. Through the years many changes had taken place in the operation of the light stations, and this house had been given up by the government and had become part of the privately owned property on Point Betsie.

To the north of us, a short city block, on a high dune the Point Betsie light stood sentinel over the cottages and Lake Michigan. The big ore boats, making their way between Chicago and Sault Sainte Marie, had been receiving light and direction from Point Betsie for well over a century. Elegant yachtsmen and hardworking fishermen set their positions by the Point Betsie light. How much comfort it has brought these many years to those who must deal realistically with the vagaries of Lake Michigan.

In the cluster of cottages, we were the only occupants. We had wanted to be away from the mainstream of life, and we had certainly accomplished that goal.

Our reverie was broken by the friendly sound of someone saying, "Welcome to Point Betsie!" We turned to see an elderly couple coming down the road. They literally reached out arms of love as they welcomed us, strangers though we were. This was our introduction to Dixon and Julia Oberdorfer, an introduction that was the beginning of a tender relationship between generations, broken only recently by death. That particular afternoon we basked in the warmth of new places and new friends. Both Blair and I were struck by the disciplined character of Julia and Dixon that permeated their lives and manifested itself in a vigor that was remarkable in a couple who had surpassed the biblical time allotted to them.

After the happy chores of unpacking were accomplished, we were invited to the Oberdorfers' for supper. Our first meal together was more than a meal—it was a sacrament. We broke bread together in the spirit of love, and all of us were aware that some quality of enduring value already existed between us.

We were impressed with the Oberdorfers' home nestled in the dunes south of the cluster of cottages. Here again was discipline and restraint. The paintings were chosen with exquisite taste; the appointments told of the extensive travels of the occupants; the books and music reflected standards of connoisseurs.

There was much to indicate the deep roots this couple had sent down—the total effect was one of order and strength—a comforting place to be in a topsy-turvy world. But more important than the things was our new friends' transcendence of the material. In this place, the spirit was dominant.

As we walked back to our cottage on that first night at Point Betsie, we were all grateful that we had found this place. The stars were brilliants set into deep velvet; the waves pounded against the beach with their steady rhythm. The wind rustled through the dunes grass so that there was a continual conclamation of nature whispering, sighing, and struggling. How right it seemed to be there. This was the beginning of something of lasting significance for the four of us—this place—the people—the church—all were to become more meaningful as the days spent there together were used as the plumb line against which all other values had to be proven.

I went to bed—lying in the darkness hearing the new sounds and I thanked God for the chance to say to these three I love: This is real—my love for you—your love for me—God's love for us.

POINT BETSIE INTERLUDE:
MYSTERY

I go down to the beach, drawn there by a sense of mystery, of timelessness. I feel the "ocean-sense" of Michigan. From *Moby Dick* come these words of Melville " ... Michigan possesses an ocean-like expansiveness, with many of the ocean's noblest traits; with many of its rimmed varieties of races and of climes." And like the lakeman Steelkilt, here I feel "wild-ocean born, and wild-ocean nurtured."

The lake has many faces. Sometimes it is a gentle face lying serene under a brilliant blue sky, throwing back the color in luminous beauty—sometimes it is restless, fussy as a naughty child, stormy and quiet by turns—and sometimes it churns and boils frighteningly under a camopy of dark clouds.

Whatever the nature of the surface, the sense of mystery is always there, like a beautiful woman whose eyes reveal something of what she's thinking, but withhold a great deal more.

I sit on the beach and watch the whitecaps far out on the lake metamorphose into huge breakers that pound against the shore. They escalate themselves onto the beach with monotonous regularity.

In you sit there long enough the rhythm of the surf and the warmth of sun and sand quiets you, a lullaby in two-part harmony that soothes and stills. As Richard of St. Victor observes, "The desirous soul no longer thirsts for God, but into God. The pull of its desire draws it into the infinite sea."

I feel drawn into the mystery of timelessness. The waves roll in on the beach, a repeat of a performance that has been going on, is going on, will be going on forever. The great sanctities of life, the past, present, and future are evident in this physical movement which has lasted millions of years.

I try to think in terms of millions. It is an impossible task. I have no experience with which to make the concept a reality. I try to fathom the love of God—it is as deep, as ineffable and myterious as the great body of water that draws the horizon.

A few vacationers are walking along the edge of the beach, their heads down. They are looking for the fossils that the waves keep bringing in, the Petoskey stone, the honeycomb, and chain. They stay close to the water's edge so they can detect the pattern of the stones as the water slaps against them.

There was a time, eons ago, when Michigan was a warm-water sea. Deep in the recesses of its waters great coral reefs were formed from the various tropical plants that grew there. Later, the glacier covered this area of America, and Lake Michigan was formed of the glacial waters. The corals fossilized and now come back to us in the quaint stones that are marked with a lovely hexagon pattern, or a distinct and crystalline chain, or a mesh of honeycomb. They draw people to the beach because they are lovely to polish, and geology and history have their own appeal.

Especially we look for the Petoskey stone. The

pattern is difficult to detect unless the stone is wet, so one either must stay close to the water's edge or—like an old pro "stoner"—lick the dry stones one suspects and see if the magic pattern appears. When polished they take on a beautiful lustrous brown shading, the hexagons appearing in a sort of crystalline outline.

From the time we discovered Point Betsie the contest to see who can find the most Petoskey stones has been raging. We have carried hundreds of stones from Michigan to Indiana, and over the years Blair emerges the victor with the keenest eye for the elusive Petoskey.

I watched as a father discovered a Petoskey. As he showed it to his son with great delight, he said, "Just think, son, this is over three hundred million years old." Three hundred million years! Does the child understand? Does the father understand? I don't! I only know it is a part of the timelessness of God. I cannot deal with the impact of such numbers—I leave that to persons who like to play with calculators.

I watched them going on with their search. The mystery attracts me. Here is evidence of change, of evolution, a distinct pattern of time, the Devonian period—pre-glacial. The evidence only deepens the mystery of creation.

Then truth overwhelms me. I am in league with the stones. With Augustine, I bow before the sovereignty of God.

"O Thou Supreme! Most secret and most present, most beautiful and strong! What shall I say, my God, my Life, my Holy Joy. What shall any man say when he speaks of Thee!"

FIRST PERSON

Space abounds here—open—unending—drawn by the curve of the dune, outlined at the far horizon of the lake—an emptiness holds you and demands introspection. Thoreau, describing another coastline, describes Point Betsie, also: "The solitude was that of the ocean and desert combined. A thousand men could not have seriously interrupted it, but would have been lost in the vastness of the scenery as their footsteps in the sand." Such a pull toward the outward scene paradoxically turns you inward.

I write about myself as a move toward Socrates' injunction to "know thyself." Or to fulfill a later similar idea expressed by Jesus, "As a man thinketh in his heart, so is he." And by means of grace the words may flow that are evidential from the heart or soul or whatever the seat of the "I" is. Right in the middle of the great identity crisis of American women I shall try to identify myself.

When Betty Friedan rent open the new women's liberation movement with the publication of her book *The Feminine Mystique,* she introduced the identity crisis of women in our culture. She said in effect that the American woman does not know who she is. She is considered an apostrophe: somebody's daughter, or somebody's wife, or somebody's mother.

I like to think of myself as much more than an apostrophe, although I happily claim all those relationships. So it is with some trepidation that I say this is the way it was with me. These are the forces that gave me growth and shape. At the same time I must say that what the forces gave growth and shape to was uniquely me—a center of being not like any other center of being in God's incredible creation. Being uniquely myself, I see the world from my own stance, and I write all this knowing that my perceptions are different from anyone else's. Still, I have set myself on this course, and I persevere.

The physical boundaries of my growing-up world were limited. There was Linn Street to the south, and the cemetery to the north—there were no east and west limits—only a knowledge that something was there I had not seen. The axis on which my small world turned ran through the Marshall County courthouse, topped by an Iowa version of Big Ben that cut my life neatly into hours. There was a centrality about the geography—Marshalltown was the center of the state: Iowa was the center of the nation; and as far as I knew the whole world revolved around the courthouse square. I was a true midwesterner—landlocked, earthbound, and satisfied. Peaks and valleys eluded me—my experience was of the flat lands of the prairies or the slightly rolling topography that Grant Wood familiarized. Earthtones—grays and browns and yellow-greens—gave serenity to the landscapes that were a part of me.

Genetically the boundaries were more interesting. On one side there was Grandpa John Plum, my mother's father. He was short, about five feet tall., but what he lacked in length, he made up in breadth, so he could not be called a small man. He was a native of the area, a child of divorce when divorce was almost unheard of. Having been on his own since the vulnerable age of nine, he had an awe-inspiring respect for childhood. He guarded his only grandchildren with care, determined that we would enjoy being young, that we would never be frightened nor hungry. He was not educated in any formal sense, but he was alert and intelligent; and his adult life had started so early and lasted so long that there were great outpourings of wisdom, subtly hidden in a morass of profanity. You had to listen carefully to get the message.

Grandpa Plum had a great zest for life—his own and everyone else's. By the time I knew him he had retired from farming; and he spent long hours with his cronies, sitting on the courthouse lawn on benches provided by the administration, so those who railed against the administration had somewhere to sit while doing so. He kept us informed as to what was happening on Main Street, and he kept Main Street informed about his grandchildren. He smoked huge cigars, drank beer, swore with abandon, and laughed.

The laughter was born somewhere deep in his girth and rolled gently at first, then convulsively, until he was rendered helpless by the spasms that shook him. Finally getting some control, the laugh would crescendo in a high breathy staccato, and almost always ended with a whack on the knee. In the circles in which I move now I hardly ever hear the good genuine

41

belly laugh that was so much a part of the sounds of my childhood.

It didn't take much to trigger this phenomenon. A good story, often as not one of his own, a child's antic, any irony of life juxtaposed against solemnity was reason enough. Before I went to school I had learned a bland little ditty from a traveling evangelist that could set Grandpa into rages of laughter. He would be playing cards with his friends, stop in the middle of the game, and say, "Now, Patty, come and sing your little song for Grandpa." Inveterate show-off that I was, I always acquiesced. Through the veil of their cigar smoke, I sang:

> Please don't smoke.
> Please don't smoke.
> Give your cigars to the billy goat.
>
> Please don't drink.
> Please don't drink.
> Booze was made for the kitchen sink.
>
> Please don't dance.
> Please don't dance.
> Jesus Christ didn't dance and prance.
>
> Please don't fight.
> Please don't fight.
> Cat and dogs make a better sight.

(Author Unknown)

Then they would begin to laugh—poor Grandpa would end by slapping his knees and wiping the tears from his eyes. I would stand there accepting the laughter, puzzled as to why they thought it was funny, waiting for the nickel or dime which would be forthcoming. Walking away, I would always hear Grandpa say, "That one—she's smart as a whip." Well maybe, but I wasn't smart enough to know what he meant.

Grandmother Plum, Grandpa's beloved "Corrie," added another dimension to my life. She was a genteel Victorian lady, with unusually beautiful skin and white hair. My sister Kate and I used to spend much time in the little Plum cottage, and she treated us regally. She prepared quaint little tea parties for her favored guests, with tiny toast sandwiches and cambric tea, and visited with us grown-up style. Her special love of Irish folklore made the fairies and leprechauns a reality for Kate and me. One of the bedtime rituals was putting out a bowl of milk for any little people who happened along.

Grandma controlled our behavior with the "fairy bowl." It was a little cut-glass bowl that sat on a high cupboard shelf. Each evening the test came—Grandma would go to the cupboard, and if we had been good little girls, the bowl contained chocolate stars that the fairies had left there. Of course, we were nearly always good, and as old and rational as I am now, I still like to savor that sense of believing in the fairies.

On the other side was Grandpa Kennedy. A giant he seemed to me then, but my father informs me that he was just a little over six feet tall. But he was big, and he had a white beard, and as far as I was concerned he was God, right out of the Old Testament, vengeful and mighty. His hands were memorable; they were the largest hands I had ever seen, and, if memory does not play tricks, I have ever seen. He was a quiet man, but authority oozed from every pore. I would have obeyed him, but he never exacted any order, only fear.

One evening he came to the house, prepared to stay for a visit of some weeks. This stands out with such clarity because we were all so out of character in his presence. The lusty, laughing life we usually indulged in was stilled, and we sat rigidly in our living room in almost total silence. A few respectful sentences from Mother and Dad about trivia, the weather, the health of our cousins and aunts and uncles, then silence. My eyes were riveted on him, on those hands folded across his knees, looking lethal in their strength, on his beard and his faded blue eyes above the whiteness. What was he thinking? I was filled with wonder. Finally he broke the silence. Pointing at me, he said sternly, "I favor her." I almost collapsed—God had blessed me.

His life was contained, so that even his children knew little about him—not the warm personal things that make the difference. I know he grew up in Sedalia, Missouri, and spent his boyhood with the likes of Jesse James and his brothers and the Daltons. But at an appropriate time he walked north to Iowa, to the small Brethren community of Ivester, to pick corn.

He worked for the Albright family, rich and powerful, sustained with sufficient moral rigor and vigor to lay a shadow over the brightest spirit. He married Kathryn Albright, the eldest child of eleven, the grandmother I never knew.

Grandfather Kennedy had great respect for his in-laws. One time at a church council session, a young man in the community took issue with a pronouncement of my great-grandmother Albright, and her son-in-law, overcome with loyalty, picked up the brother and bodily removed him from the church. Pax.

Not being a birthright Brethren, Grandfather

Kennedy did not understand the nuances of this way of life. On the first Christmas following his marriage he presented his in-laws with a set of hollowware. The gift was returned, with much moralizing about the simple life. He never gave another gift to anyone in his long life.

It would not be right to exclude three women whose lives had certain immeasurable effects on mine. They were my three great aunts: Aunt Mae and Aunt Tibby Albright and a married sister, Aunt Ida Wolfe. These women were birthright Brethren, exemplifying Brethren values of simplicity and caring as a way of life. Their physical setting was a richly endowed farm in central Iowa near the Ivester Church of the Brethren, and from this central point their sphere of influence reached out to many, especially their nieces and nephews and great nieces and great nephews.

They dressed simply—having no thought of being fashionable nor of using money in any way that did not embody hard-rock pragmatism. Aesthetics eluded them although they believed in and encouraged (with the most practical kind of help—money) their young relatives to go to college.

Growing up in the depression, we did not have access to vacation spots or travel experiences. But we did go to our aunts' "farm." Looking back on this experience, I do not know if they wanted us to come or if our parents wanted us to go. I only know my sisters and I went to the farm almost every summer, and there the aunts' moral vigor found its way into our bones. Their only expletive was the word "sugar!" We couldn't have soft drinks because beer was sold in bottles, and there seemed to be some connection.

Dancing was sacrilege. Work was highly virtuous; the harder you worked, the better you were. But there was fun and lessons to be learned from watching and listening.

If there was sickness or trouble at home one of the great aunts would appear. Suddenly leftovers could be stretched out indefinitely, you could survive with using very little electricity—our way of life altered subtly but surely. And there was always that sense that we could never be quite as good as they expected us to be—that somehow the whole family fell just a little short of the expectations of these three paragons.

These were the roots close to the ground that I could see. They went deep into an admixture of cultures and faiths and types—but one thing was obvious. In spite of the dichotomy, the fruit borne by the roots was terribly strong. These people who were important to me were the stuff of the frontier, physically rugged and mentally agile. And above all else, they knew who they were.

THE PEOPLE

To try to pick up the chief threads that make the whole cloth is both a difficult and enjoyable task—as you seek to sort out, and cast aside, and bring back again those chief things that make your life.

There were people and there was a time, there were places and things.

There is my father, Roy Kennedy. He inherited from his father a commanding physical presence. He was born into the simple-lived Brethren who had accumulated impressive land holdings in central Iowa. When the land and the fortune it represented were lost, my father was left to the devices of his intuition and his wit. He was a cattleman—buying and selling livestock, trying to beat the market. His physical prowess was deceptive—under the brawn beat a sensitive heart, out of the stern face came a beautiful voice, and his large hands moved over the keyboard with ease, in response to his perfect ear for music.

He had a rare gift—the grateful heart. Through all the difficult and uncertain times of the depression, of serious illness, of personal loss, he remained grateful for the blessings of love, of food, of his family and his faith. Now at the age of seventy-five he is almost blind, but he remains grateful for the beauty he has seen. As age overtakes him this gratefulness is expanded so that he sees every day as a gift from God, and even the smallest extension of another human being to him is granted a spiritual dimension by the appreciation it evokes.

He made my world safe. At times his sternness frightened me, but I relied heavily upon him for protection of all kinds, and it was granted and is still granted.

Mother was Julia Plum before she married Dad. She was a registered nurse par excellence, and it was in this capacity that her and Dad's paths were destined to cross. Dad's first wife had died in the influenza epidemic following the first World War, and he was left with an infant daughter, Lois.

When Lois was twenty months of age she became very ill. The family doctor in the village of Steamboat Rock urged Dad to get Lois to a hospital. So he bundled his baby up, boarded a train and traveled to Marshalltown. Near midnight the train arrived at its destination, and he hurried Lois through the winter darkness to the Deaconess Hospital.

A Deaconess sister met him in the spacious receiving room. When she saw the dying child, she hurriedly called Dr. French, an eminent eye and ear specialist. Dr. French unhesitatingly explained that Lois had a double mastoiditis and informed Dad that he would operate on her the first thing in the morning.

Then the doctor contacted my mother and urged her to come and take care of the child. Mother declined, stating that she had been on mastoid cases all winter and she was weary of such demanding care. Dr. French prevailed saying, "Julia, this is a very sad case. It's a young widower who refuses to leave the child for a moment. He hasn't slept for several days. It won't last long, I'm sure, for I see no hope of her surviving."

So Mother came and took over Lois' life, giving her the intensive care that such an illness called for in the pre-antibiotic days. Lois survived and Dr. French placed the credit directly in my mother's loving ministry to her. Following this crisis meeting, of trusting his dying child to a stranger's care, Dad was never able to be without Julia.

Our family never tired of hearing this story for it gave to our parents' meeting the drama and romance in which we delighted. We also loved to hear it because Lois was our oldest sister, a tower of strength, our captain courageous; and we shuddered when we considered what life would have been like without her.

Mother was the kind of woman who invited envy in others because her capabilities and talents had such range and scope. Her nursing career had endowed her with a sense of order and efficiency. Along with that she was deeply sensitive to all aspects of beauty, to art and music. She sewed like a professional, and in the worst days of the depression we remained decently dressed because of her skill and resourcefulness. She read widely, expressed herself with clarity, and was possessed of a certain pride that made respect the natural response. Never in her whole life has she given way to what Willa Cather describes as "that part of her which would set up an idol, or that part of her which would bow down to it." These basic human values of self-worth and respect for the worth of others are a major part of her children's value systems.

She presented to us a beautiful example of how to love a man deeply, care diligently for his creature comforts, run a home, and in the midst of life's holocaust to remain one's own person. Her temper was phenomenal—to be on the receiving end was catastrophic—but Julia has to be seen whole instead of in parts.

If Dad was a protector, Mother was a haven. Her softness shielded me from the hardness of life— teachers were hard, and situations were hard, and growing up was hard—but Julia was soft and compassionate, willing to hold her children in her arms and willing to take their side in their little battles. All good things—warm houses, the smell of fresh-baked bread, a clean starched dress, loving words, shared dreams, iced drinks, special care during illness—all good things came from Julia in a flowing stream of love.

And they continue to come—beautiful gifts from the kiln and the loom, lovely sweaters and mittens off Grandma's knitting needles, encouraging and insightful letters, and, above all, the knowledge that the haven is still there. When the way seems too hard there is softness.

By nature, organizations eluded Mother. Her creativity could not find expression in the little confines of women's clubs, and unless she was at the hospital on a special case she was at home. Availability was one of her chief virtues, not only to her family but to her friends. And friends were drawn to her for the cup of tea which was in reality a cup of cold water in Christ's name. A visit with Julia was therapeutic, and there were many patients—the neighbors, her nurse friends, the relatives. I grew up among "visitors"—the satisfaction of the conversation "a deux" remains my chief indulgence in life.

My oldest sister Lois, half-sister in blood and whole sister in every other way, gave a stability to my life. Lois was eight years older than I, and I assumed her presence and help with the same unconscious faith I assumed light and shadow would follow darkness.

And Kathryn, called Kate, who preceded me into the family circle by only twenty months, was as close as my right arm, and as necessary and useful. Life without her would have been untenable, for she introduced me to the intricacies of childhood games, held my hand when we crossed streets or walked through the woods, taught me to dress myself, to tie my shoes, and in every way made herself so indispensable that a short absence from her created a well of loneliness that could only be filled with her reappearance.

Up to the time I was eight years old, the major event in my life had been the birth of our brother Joseph Winston Kennedy. Joe was born on an early morning of a lovely Sunday in June in 1932. Although I was nearly seven years old then, his arrival came as a complete shock to me. The only evidence that I recall as any awareness on my part of a change in my mother was that I requested her not to accompany me on our trips to the library for—I hesitated to tell her—she was too fat.

I remember the sense of elation with which my father told us three girls about the arrival of our brother. I remember a fleeting thought—was everyone this happy when I was born? But such thoughts were soon swept away in the delight of getting ready to go to the hospital to see Joey. After a walk of about a mile, we arrived just as they were allowing visitors in. Hospital visiting rules were not so stringent then, so we all crowded into Mother's room, and the nurse brought our red and squirming brother to us.

We planned to stay the whole day as we were too far from home to go back and forth freely. At noon we went out to forage for lunch. It would never have occurred to us to find a restaurant for that would cost too much. But we found a grocery store and Dad bought a big sack of bananas and a quart of ice cream. The grocer gave us some wooden spoons, and we sat on the hospital lawn and celebrated our brother's birth.

Every afternoon for a week, Lois, Kate, and I made the long walk to the St. Thomas Hospital to see our darling mother and the new baby. Then the special day came when they arrived home, and the family was a complete and charmed circle, which has not been broken yet.

So welcomed was Joseph into a household of females that his early years were spent in a chaos of fighting over who was to care for him, which of us could dress him, could rock him, could wheel his carriage. Kate and I went so far as to have a tug-of-war with him, she pulling his arms and I his legs in an effort to show our wonderful love. His proud father moved in quickly to save him from our violent affections. In spite of such beginnings he has developed into a quite normal human being.

These were the people who molded and shaped me, who argued with me, fought with me, protected me, taught me to be human, and cushioned me for life with layers of love.

THE TIME

To write about myself or the Kennedy family without setting us in a specific time would be a lack of integrity. We could be seen whole only as we lived through those crucial depression years, which lasted for us from the late twenties until the early forties, when the war economy asserted itself.

It must be to the credit of my parents, to their resilience and special brand of faith, that we lived through the depression less aware of the bleakness of our situation than seems possible in retrospect. My father had known wealth, and my mother had been a career woman for some years previous to her marriage. Both of them had an inherent pride that gave them a certain toughness during those rugged years. I can only thank God for the greatness of my parents' spirits as they prevailed daily over our lives during those stringent times.

It is difficult, writing this in the midst of an unbelievably affluent culture, to ascertain how they did so well. Dad was unskilled and worked at a variety of selling jobs. Since no one had any money with which to buy anything, what small success he did enjoy assumed the proportions of miracles.

At one time Dad worked as a car salesman. His pay

was on a commission basis, and since no one had any money to buy cars, it is not difficult to imagine the plight in which he found himself. Some evenings the garage owner would give him a quarter or a dime—a miserable offering—and he would bring it home. But in those days it was enough for a loaf of bread and a quart of milk, and we never went hungry.

Dad was selling cars in the winter of 1933, and Mother had been ill and unable to work. Lois and Kate both babysat and did little jobs for the neighbors, and all the money went unquestioningly into the family fund. The outlook for Christmas seemed very bleak—my mother always made great celebrations for us, but this year there would be no tree or gifts. Mentally they tried to prepare us for our lack, but we were all visionaries and knew what we would have Christmas.

Just a few days before Christmas Dad's boss told him of an elderly man who might be in the market for a new car, so Dad called on this prospect hoping against hope that he would sell a car before Christmas. The gentleman invited him in, and as they began to visit he said to Dad, "Are you one of the Kennedy boys from the Ivester Church?" Dad assured him that he was. The old man persisted, "Are you one of the Kennedy boys that sing so well?" Dad modestly agreed that he was.

The man then told Dad that his wife had been sick for a long time and that it would cheer her up if she could hear some Christmas carols. So Dad, who can play by ear any song he has heard, sat down at the piano and sang all the carols he knew; and she wanted more, so he sang all the old familiar hymns. His repertoire was not small. For over two hours he played and sang, and the old man bought a car. So we had Christ-mas—the tree, the presents, the trimmings. With such collective faith as we had, miracles could be assumed.

In truth, I must say it was Mother's resourcefulness as a manager that saved us. Her skill as a seamstress was taxed during those years, because even the ac-coutrements for sewing were hard to come by. She would haunt rummage sales and buy garments that still had good material in them, laboriously rip them apart, and start all over again, cutting and synthesizing the old into the new. Her pride would not allow her to send her children out looking like ragamuffins.

Even her wedding dress went the way of the shears and needles to make Lois a blouse in which she could perform with the high school trio. None of us was allowed to touch the sewing machine or her tools, in-cluding the scissors, because too much depended on their availability and usefulness.

For years we went to sleep to the lullaby of the old treadle machine. When we awoke a new garment would be hanging in the doorway between the dining room and living room. Miracles surrounded us. Mother clothed us, all except my father, from the skin out. For her the practical solution was not sufficient; it had to be aesthetic. Consequently, we were the poorest kids imaginable with the best-dressed look. I'm afraid our shoes gave us away, since Mother could not make them for us; but from the ankles up we looked great.

The most negative aspect of those years was what the worry and frustration did to the folks' relationship. There was never any doubt that they loved each other deeply, but their emotions gave way under the strain of care, and I recall a great deal of conflict between them during that period. I think if poor finances had not entered the picture, my parents would have had an almost idyllic marriage. Dad adored Mother, and his tender and romantic attitude toward her was touching. I have seen him come into a noise-filled house at the end of the day, with all four of his children contributing to same; yet, if Mother was gone, he would ask, "Where is everybody?" As long as his Julie was absent, everyone was absent.

In return for such devotion, Mother paid great attention to his creature comforts, preparing his favorite foods, having the house in readiness for his homecoming, gearing her day to that moment when he would return. I have memories of waking up from an afternoon nap, warm and fuzzy with sleep, being greeted by Mother saying, "Come now, we must get all cleaned up for Daddy." It was a ritual for Kate and me; we would present ourselves shining and ready for Julie's liege, lord, and master.

The positive thing about those years was the cohesive effect the situation had on our family. We were contained. There was no money for travel, for entertainment, for club dues, for music lessons, for girl scout uniforms, no money—period, so we stayed home. We read to each other, we sang, we worked, we visited. I think it could be said truthfully that we talked our way through the depression.

My folks never left us to go out to dinner or go to a movie or to do anything just for fun. Except that there was one night a week when they left us in charge of Lois and walked up town to Bank Night. Bank Night was a cultural phenomenon that had arrived with the depression. Great crowds would gather outside the theatre, waiting anxiously for the drawing of the winning ticket. You had to be present to claim the money. The folks couldn't afford to buy tickets to the show, so they waited with the huddled masses in rain and sleet and snow and heat, hoping somehow the magic moment might arrive when their name would be called. And we waited anxiously at home to see if we had become rich instantaneously. It never happened, but we lived in hope.

Mother's description of us was "the sassy poor." She explained to us that this meant we were without funds but not without pride, self-respect, and intelligence. We ate depression food at an humble but orderly table—depression food being flour gravy, stewed tomatoes, boiled potatoes, and other such fare. One evening we sat down to a meal of graham mush, and then began the meal on this note. Roy speaking: "We don't have much to eat tonight, but we've got each other—we've got our health—we've got smart kids." And then with a sigh, "A man can't ask for much more."

Perhaps we missed the bleak note of the times because we were always surrounded by books and music. We were all constant readers, and we were all natural musicians, Mother being a proficient pianist as well as Dad. We usually had a piano but not always. If things got too bad, we'd sell the piano; and the first time any money was available we'd buy another one. Pianos moved in and out of our lives like restless relatives.

High points occurred when Grandma and Grandpa Plum would appear with huge sacks of groceries. Or Grandpa would invite us to go downtown with him and he would get new shoes for us. On rare occasions they took us to the movies. After hearing Paul Robeson sing "Old Man River" in *Showboat,* Grandpa decided Roy and Julie must have that experience, and the next evening they walked to town, out of their drab lives momentarily.

Shining out of those dark years was a light that was constant. It was the light of faith that radiated from my parents' lives, expressed in different ways, but always shimmering over us and pointing us in a specific direction.

It is odd to think that during those years Mother and Dad did not attend church. They disobeyed the maxim, "Take your children to church. Don't send them." They sent us. Dad didn't go because, as a birthright Brethren, he felt denominational loyalty. Since the Church of the Brethren was fifteen miles away and we were unmechanized, that settled the question for him. Mother didn't go because, having had a reputation for being a beautifully dressed woman, her lack of lovely clothes limited her activities. For some years she did not go about much, and when she went out again it was in the style in which she chose to go.

But the believing was present. Living was an act of faith. My father's theme song was "His Eye Is on the Sparrow and I Know He Watches Me." How often I've heard him sing it, and how much he believed it. Mother seemed aware of the great mysteries of life. Brooding, her deep dark eyes sad and visionary, she'd say, "We don't need to understand. We just need to know it will be all right." And then, mysteriously, "One must believe. It is the only way."

I think at that time in her life Mother got great

satisfaction in material that came from a group called Unity. Pamphlets and leaflets arrived by mail and the reading of them seemed to buoy her up and sustain her. I don't know how much of this she shared with Dad, but she taught me Unity's Prayer of Faith, and for most of my childhood it daily attended me.

> God is my help in every need;
> God does my every hunger feed;
> God walks beside me, guides my way
> Through every moment of the day.
>
> I now am wise, I now am true,
> Patient, kind, and loving, too:
> All things I am, can do, and be,
> Through Christ, the truth that is in me.
>
> God is my health, I can't be sick;
> God is my strength, unfailing, quick;
> God is my all, I know no fear,
> Since God and love and truth are here.
>
> *Unity School of Christianity*
> *Kansas City, Missouri*

I believed. When did I not believe? Never that I can consciously remember. The quality of my belief has matured, but I have never not believed. How did God come to me? From Dad's songs, from Mother's brooding face? From some obscure Sunday school teacher, from the church? Or did the Holy Spirit, with a "bright flash of wing" I missed seeing, invade my heart? I don't know. I only "know Whom I have believed," and for this gift of faith I return joy in full measure.

THE PLACES

Three places made a difference in my growing-up days. School was not one of them. School was not a focus of attention for me, even though it was time consuming. I wandered through school in a dream state, living in my own world of thought, tuning in often enough to be responsive. In retrospect, I think I was educated by osmosis. My pores must have soaked up what knowledge I had, because my mind and spirit were invariably elsewhere. Even college was an experience I lived through without much consciousness of the formal work involved. I majored in extra-curricular activities and people, and my own private reading was always more important than textbooks.

The library was my home away from home. I established squatter's rights at a very tender age and harassed an assortment of librarians for years. I can't remember learning to read. I can remember being very put out with my fellow first graders who had to be taught that skill. I read aloud a great deal in the early days of my schooling. I know now it was to give the teachers a rest. Miss Pierce and Miss Currier would say, "Now, Patty, you read." And they blanked out while I displayed my virtuosity with those twenty-six symbols which gave some of my peers so much trouble.

The summer following my first year of school I was allowed to go to the library alone. The ritual of getting ready, of walking down the shady streets dotted with patches of gold, of knowing what lay ahead, filled me with delight. Suddenly the huge stone edifice came into sight. I usually got there before the library opened, and I would sit on the big cement balustrade, the sun shining in my face, waiting for Miss O'Connor to arrive and turn the key to unlock that symbolic door to the world of books. She never seemed particularly happy to see me, but my joy was dependent on the commodity instead of her. I would follow her up the stairs, inhaling that unique library smell of books and binding, paper and paste, and ascend to the children's floor.

We were allowed to take three books at a time. I would choose mine and run home. Usually by early afternoon I would be back at the library, blandly greeting Miss O'Connor, who grew more perplexed with every encounter.

After about two weeks of this I was through the second- and third-grade shelves, working diligently away on books for older children. I annoyed Miss O'Connor. One morning, after I had been waiting for her and was silently admitted into her juvenile domain, she followed me to the shelves. She took a book from the fifth-grade section and handed it to me rather roughly. "Now," she said, "Read!" Her command startled me, but I opened the book and, goaded a little by fright, I read so fast she had trouble following me. Finally she said, "That's enough."

That was the beginning of a strange friendship. I was no longer an intruder who didn't belong. I was a sister under the skin. My reading was no hoax. I had gained Miss O'Connor's respect, and with it came smiles and help in selecting the books she thought I would most enjoy. Oh, the joy of that best-of-all-possible-worlds—the world of books.

Thus began a pilgrimage that was to be lifelong—the utter fascination of the printed page. One of the great mysteries of my life is why everyone does not love to read. People have tried to explain it to me, but my bond with books is evidently organic in nature. I pity those not likewise arranged.

Eventually I graduated to the main library level and voraciously read Gothic novels, biographies, whatever I could lay my hands on. I established some kind of record when, at the age of thirteen, I was the first person at the library to check out the long awaited copy of "Gone With the Wind." When I got into adult books that took more than one morning to read, a failing of mine came to light. Once I had possession of a book for long, it became mine. I could not give it up until my family was aware of the fines due and I was forced to return what was mine in spirit. Returning books I loved made me feel dispossessed.

I would run up more fines than I could possibly pay. Then the kindly librarian, who seemed to understand my obsession, would lead me to the basement of the library. Among the paste pots and new books, I would do penance for my sin by pasting the due-date notices in the books. Oh, the delight of my penance! They were my books. Working in "my library" was a perfect punishment for my delicious crime of keeping books too long.

My reading life, begun in the Marshalltown Library, which seems much smaller now that I am grown, is still an essential part of me. To think of a long evening ahead without something good to read can throw me into a panic. I still put biographies and autobiographies at the top of my list, but if everything else fails, I'll read cereal boxes and gum wrappers. Hell, to me, would be any place without a printing press.

Some children play in parks—some choose school yards—Kate and I chose the Marshalltown cemetery. We moved a lot but stayed in the same end of town, always near the cemetery. We believed it to be one of the most beautiful cemeteries in the world, and there was something idyllic about it. In the center was an enticing pond with a flowing fountain that caught the rainbow over and over again as the water cascaded downward.

On the pond were exquisitely graceful swans and fluffy ducks waiting for us to arrive with dry bread to feed them. Skirting the water was a variety of trees, but our special tree was a weeping willow, one low branch of which hung over the pond. Kate and I would climb onto it, sit among the graceful leaves, hidden from the world; and we would watch the swans, the people, and our own distorted reflections. We would visit in low muffled tones. The place demanded reverence.

According to legend there were more varieties of trees for a given space in our cemetery than for any other comparable space in the world. We walked endlessly gathering leaves and acorns—checking the legend to be sure, making our own legends.

We had one relative buried there. We referred to

him respectfully as Uncle Charlie. He was my mother's brother and had died in infancy, so we had never known him as an uncle. But we would visit his simple grave, sit quietly, and talk about him as if we had known him well. His loss seemed important.

We had unspoken rules about the cemetery. We never went alone. We never walked over a grave. We never went near a freshly dug grave. And we never picked a single flower off a freshly decorated grave. Death was something we walked around, not something that would come to us. We were immortal—yet we did talk in hushed voices; and, when the shadows of the tombstones began to fall a certain way, we turned toward home, walking faster and faster till we were outside the huge iron gates.

But we always went back. For the birds and the trees, the swans and the flowers, the marble and granite, the statue of the big elk, the grave of the World War I veteran, the huge cross in the Catholic section with Jesus looking so twisted and tortured, the thorns so cruel—all these symbols beckoned us.

And one thing filled us with fear. At the far fringe of the cemetery, dug into the side of the hill, was a little cave where the tools and machines were kept. We started going to the cemetery when we were very young. Coming upon this cave one day, with its iron-barred entrance, we decided it was the abode of the devil. Having once decided this, no amount of reason could persuade us otherwise. We were drawn to the cave—not close—but near enough to look in awe and fear, lest the devil be waiting for us. One day Kate got brave enough to yell, "Hey, devil—come out!" But as soon as her voice reverberated against the hollow opening, we started running and kept running until we could see home.

After Joe was born we would wheel him in his pram, and our destination was always the cemetery. We would take dried bread along to feed the swans—wheel the carriage as close to the waters' edge as we dared, and let our baby brother enjoy the closeness of those beautiful creatures. One day he seemed content in his carriage—it was the old-fashioned wicker kind that had a dropped section so the baby could sit up and his feet would hang down. Kate and I ventured into our willow tree, intending to watch Joe from above. But, of course, we momentarily forgot our charge. Suddenly Kate screamed. Joe had gotten out of the pram and walked into the pond. Only his head was visible. We commanded him to stay where he was, and we bustled in among the startled swans to effect a rescue.

We wheeled our soaking wet baby brother home— with great speed—and it was some time before we were entrusted with his care again.

For years that was our chief playground. The richest child was never surrounded with more beauty. Our life in the midst of death gave us a superior feeling. Yet the knowledge of death filled us with wonder and an unspoken fear. That is the one place that seems unchanged to me when I return home. Walking through the big gates gives me an eerie sense of walking back into childhood—the pond, the weeping willow, the elk, Christ on the cross. Are even the swans the same?

My first memory of the church is a strange mixture of sights and sounds and odors. There was the delicious smell of beef that had been cooked a long time; there was the sight of many relatives, the great-aunts in white bonnets that tied under their chins, aunts and cousins in small white prayer coverings; the sight of my mother, conforming, yet somehow removed and apart from what was happening. Added to this were the comforting sounds of Dad's rich bass voice rising and falling with a natural reverence and the sense of communion as the congregation sang richly harmonized hymns.

The occasion was a Brethren love feast. I was very small, but I knew it was a replica of events of the Last Supper. The Brethren knelt and washed one another's feet as Jesus had washed Peter's feet. The Brethren ate a common meal together as the disciples had eaten together. Toward that end the beef had cooked all day in big kettles, filling the church with an odor that was to stay with me forever—a strange beckoning to reverence. I could not take part in the sacraments, since I was not yet baptized. But Julia saw that that delicious beef and broth was shared with her wondering child.

It seems fitting that this memory of the church should be so graphic to me, because the Brethren faith was my heritage. I was to drift in to and out of it for years, but I was never to forget that my birthright was this pious, simple-lived people who had no creed but the New Testament and who reenacted the Last Supper twice a year. The feet washing was an act of humility, the meal an act of fellowship, and the eucharist was that high sacrament of symbolically taking on the nature of Christ.

Since there was no Church the Brethren in Marshalltown, during the depression years in our unmechanized state we Kennedys aligned ourselves with different denominations. We enjoyed a strange religious freedom and a variety of religious experiences that made our white-bonneted great-aunts certain we were on the road to hell.

Kate and I at different times were Baptists, German Lutherans, and Disciples of Christ. We would have liked to have been Roman Catholic just long enough to get a good look at their stained glass windows, the most magnificent in town. We steered clear of the Methodists, there being so many of them that we were sure they didn't "need us." Now I know nobody particularly needed us. The wheels of Protestantism could move without depending upon the presence of two little girls, each bearing one penny and each with an unexplained eagerness to be a part of organized religion.

The strangest year we had was our year with the German Lutherans. It was a tiny church—we chose it because a neighborhood friend went there and liked her Sunday school teacher. In spite of the small congregation there were two services—an early service where German was spoken and sung, then Sunday school, and then a service performed in English. Kate and I would always go to Sunday school early and slip in in the middle of the German service. Fascinated by a strange tongue, we would listen to the preacher intently, unable to understand a word, but an eerie sensitivity to the Spirit's presence filled us. It was as if we were in the midst of a great baptism of the Holy Spirit— everyone but ourselves speaking in strange tongues. I think it was in that little German church that the universality of Christ became real to us.

But it was to the Disciples that we gave our chief allegiance. Lois was deeply involved in the program for young people and was the best soprano in the choir. Her clear, bell-like voice comforted me in the midst of strangers. Kate sometimes joined me in the congregation, but often I was by myself.

I chose a pew in the balcony overlooking the whole panorama of churchliness. I sang lustily; I listened intently. It was during those years of solitude in the midst of services that I developed habits that have always stayed with me. I enjoyed listening to, rather than participating in, any unison prayers or reading. I learned there was a certain cadence to the gathered church, and surrounded by the sound of voices rising and falling together, of praising God, and the breathiness of the final a-men, I had a religious experience. I still listen to that special cadence, filled with certainty that the "kingdoms of this world shall become the kingdom of our Lord." I discovered I enjoyed being alone. Solitude allowed me the attention I desired to give—was this my first "divine attentiveness" to God?

The minister of the Disciples church made a strong impact on my life, though I'm sure he was not aware of it. He was a forceful preacher, a picture of decorum in his swallowtail coat. As was customary in the Disciples church, he gave the invitation at the close of every service.

One Sunday, when I was ten years old, I had been especially moved by the total service—the choir, the minister's preaching—and when he intoned the invitation, I had a distinct sense that it was a personal call to me. The congregation was singing, "I'll go where you want me to go, dear Lord. I'll be what you want me to be." The message was clearly for me. Just as I slipped out of my place in the pew, I caught a fleeting glimpse of the look of disbelief on Lois' face. I walked resolutely down that long center aisle. I stood in front of the congregation while the pastor laid his hands on my head and reminded his flock that "a little child" shall lead them.

Lois and Kate knew we were Brethren—they knew that sooner or later I had to be baptized three times forward, in the name of the Father, Son, and the Holy Ghost. But the call had come to me. I only did publicly what I had felt so long privately. A small and poor vessel I was, but I belonged to Christ. I would go through the water, once backward for the Disciples, three times forward for the Brethren. It was of little import—what mattered was that I felt personally aligned to Christ, his goodness and his light.

We three were very solemn on the way home. Lois and Kate informed me I was "really going to get it," although I'm not certain what punishment they thought fitting for "hitting the sawdust trail." Kate got there first, proclaiming irreverently, "Patty joined the church, and we couldn't stop her." Dad made some remark to the effect that we had to get a car (which would turn us into Brethren) and Mother seemed to think it was the most natural thing in the world. She put her arm around me and said to all of them, "Patty has always belonged to the church." My parents made one of their rare appearances at the Disciples church to be present at my first baptism.

Two services at the Disciples church stand out with clarity. One Sunday morning the pastor invited us to be present that evening if we wished to be part of an unusual experience. I coaxed Lois into taking me, because I couldn't go alone at night. When we arrived at the church, I was struck by the presence of a huge black box in front of the altar. "What is it? What is it?" I kept asking Lois. "It's a coffin—now hush."

A coffin—I was terribly uneasy during the service. The minister talked about people who are spiritually dead—and I pitied them. At the end of the service, he stepped foward and said solemnly, "We will now view the body." The congregation moved forward, a total silence adding a quality of fear to the situation. Lois pushed me along— I had coaxed to come, hadn't I? When we got to the coffin, we had a startling experience. The minister had rigged a mirror, so that as you passed by you saw yourself. It was a weird sensation, but it worked for me. At least, I vowed never to be among that huge company of the spiritually dead.

I'm sure not everyone looked with favor upon the minister's tactics. I recall my folks' chagrin. It may have been in questionable taste, but, oh, it was a memorable Sunday evening.

The other service that is engraved in my very soul was my first sunrise service. The thought of getting up before the sun rose on Easter morning filled me with elation. Lois and Kate and I went proudly through our early Sabbath town. This was the day that the Lord had made. Oh, sweet belief!

When we entered the church we were greeted by unforgettable sights and sounds. On the altar were between twenty and thirty bird cages, filled with singing canaries. The organist was playing triumphant music. For forty minutes we sat there, entranced with

71

the birds singing as though their throats would burst, while the organist greeted the dawn with canticles of praise and victory. The sun streamed through the windows, the canaries sang, strains of the "Hallelujah Chorus" reverberated through the sanctuary. Christ is risen, he is risen, indeed! I thought my heart would burst. It was too small for such ecstasy.

Of course, the day came when we got a car, and the Brethren beckoned us impatiently. The Disciples pastor was furious with our folks for removing us from his fold. Evidently he did need us. But I slipped naturally and easily into the Brethren pattern. I was re-baptized—three times forward in the name of the Father, the Son, and the Holy Ghost. However, nothing was really altered because I had that "joy, joy, joy down in my heart." The name I attached to it was immaterial.

POINT BETSIE INTERLUDE:
SILENCE

At Point Betsie there is a magnificent silence in the dunes that draws one into them. Such silence demands a kind of reverence—it is a herald of prayer.

I went into the dunes, climbed them, and explored them for various reasons. Sometimes such a prosaic motive as getting a good tan sent me into them. Occasionally I climbed the steepest dunes I could find just for the benefit of the exercise I would get, the sheer muscular challenge of the sand.

Or sometimes a treasure hunt inspired me—the treasure of the wind wood. Eons before Point Betsie had a name, a large forest bordered the lake. In God's good time the sand moved in on it, piled up around those stately trees, and literally buried the forest. I found pieces of the wind wood, in haunting and grotesque shapes, silvered and smoothly polished by the relentless activity of time, the winds and sand smoothing and shaping them into objects of beauty.

The search for wild flowers took me into the dunes. Their lovely faces lifted up out of the sand in defiance of their environment. Their roots must have gone very deep to find the water that gave them life. There was the wild gentian and wild sweet pea, the tiny bluebell whose size makes its hardiness seem surprising, and the exquisite Star of Bethlehem, perfectly shaped.

But whatever purpose sent me there, the result was always the same. The silence caught me, held me by its mysterious power, rocketed me into the life of the spirit, even though I fully intended to address myself to lesser pursuits.

I had left behind a noisy world. The ringing of the telephone, the sonorous melody of the door bell, the whining of the vacuum cleaner, the grinding of the garbage disposal, the combined sounds of the washing machine and drier, the furnace turning on and off at the thermostat's electrical demand, the overpowering voice of television—all the things that were supposed to make my life easier but mainly increased the volume of sound were far away.

Outside our home there was incessant activity of traffic, the multifarious sounds of the mechanical world, the screeching of brakes, honking of horns, gunning of engines, the clang and the beep and the whistle, all distracting us from any center of thought.

And there was the mismanagement of music. At the dentist's there was "music to drill by"; at the doctor's "music to wait by"; at the supermarket "music to shop by"; at the restaurant "music to eat by." Even lovely sounds, indiscriminately and irreverently used, become noise.

Small wonder that silence so deep, so penetrating as that in the dunes startles you, if you are a part of this "age of noise." Inevitably, I became very still, very quiet, not daring to intrude on this miracle of silence. Like Moses, I discovered that the place where I stood was holy ground; reverence was the spontaneous response.

Thomas a Kempis said, "Silence is the nutriment of devotion." There in the dunes my soul was fed in such a way that my thoughts spiraled upwards. The admonition of Paul to "pray without ceasing" seemed to present no problem. For in the midst of such penetrating silence only one attitude seemed natural, and that was the attitude of prayer. Even if I wanted to remain earthbound, I could not in such mystical surroundings. My heart soared upward, gave itself over completely to a spiritual communion that defied the working of the mind. I found myself following the advice a dear mother had given her son. When he asked her how to pray, she said, "Praise Him and thank Him, praise Him and thank Him."

In the silence of the dunes my heart was always full. There were so many reasons to "praise Him and thank Him." Praise God for the beauty with which he surrounds us. Praise God for the pattern of creation that emerges more sharply as men and women become more knowledgeable. Praise God for the revelation of his nature, his willingness to become human, to walk among us so that we might come to understand that God is love.

Thank God for life. To be alive, aware, to breathe and see and feel, to grow humbly but hopefully in his image. Thank God for the people who touch us in loving and caring ways. Thank God that we can love.

Thank God for this silence which makes the soul captive. I must go back into the world of noise, but by the alchemy of grace the quietness of the dunes becomes a part of me.

When I go to the dunes I wrap myself in silence and wait. Simone de Weil's phrase "divine attentiveness to God" becomes experience instead of words. I wait and listen. "How silently, how silently, the wondrous gift is given."

ON COMING OF AGE

One prevalent motif dominated my early life. It was a motif of idealistic optimism—the shining sense that everything was getting better and better every day in every way.

We were poor—we would be rich. We were waiting at the dock—the wait would be worthwhile—our ship would come in. There had been wars—there would be no more wars. People had been barbarous—people were getting increasingly kinder, more loving. All the good things of the world would be brought to bear upon humanity, so that in the end—some "end" that I would still be around to see—righteousness would prevail.

Dad was an optimist. Anyone who didn't have a dime in his pocket or a dollar in his hand, who had four children and a wife and maintained a happy spirit, a shining eye, and a great singing voice must be an optimist. If Mother did not believe in waiting for the elusive ship, she kept her grim thoughts hidden.

And in the reading that had consumed so much of my life there were heroes. There were those bright and shining boys in the Alger books, the ones who climbed from rags to riches in fifteen chapters, never failing to assert the power of right over every vicissitude life offered. There were the beloved biographies: Florence Nightingale, symbol of love and charity; Clara Barton, striding among the soldiers, healing the broken, binding up the wounded; Jane Addams, single-handedly transforming the slums of Chicago; Jenny Lind, poor little girl with no direction, singing to her cat. But suddenly the cat is transformed to an audience of kings and queens, all bowing before her gift. Oh, one could overcome!

My alter egos—my beckoning lights they were. I would build a greater than Hull House. I would offer something to the world so spectacular that kings and queens would bow before me, although I would only bow to Christ the King. How sustaining fantasy can be.

The question of war nagged at me, though the only war that was contemporary with my early childhood was the Spanish Civil War. One morning my father took me outside and pointed eastward to a red sunrise. The sun itself was not visible, just a red vapor that hung against the horizon. "See the red sky?" he asked. "It's a sign of the war. They started fighting in Spain." "Why is it a sign of the war?" I asked. "Because men's red blood will be shed." I did not question his conclusion.

My father had served with the American Expeditionary Forces in World War I, and some hatred of war had been born in us through his experience. It was not that he verbalized it. In the old photograph album we could see the pictures of his company on a boat at Liverpool. The Palace at Versailles was the background of another picture, the men looking casual but smart in their uniforms. And on every possible occasion the flag flew from our porch, the flag Dad had been presented when he received his honorable discharge. We treated it with reverence. Dad told us only one story, and that was of his homecoming. He told how the big troop ship arrived in the harbor at New York early one morning, and how the sun glanced so brilliantly off the Statue of Liberty. When he saw her, so splendid and proud, he cried like a baby and vowed never to leave his native soil again. It was an utter impossibility for me to imagine him crying, though I believed him.

Several times during my childhood, nights were shattered by almost animal-like moans and then a pierced scream, and then quiet. I would snuggle up fearfully to Kate or Lois, and they would whisper that Dad was having his war dream. When I questioned my mother, she explained to me about shell shock, something about an exploding ammunition dump, and how occasionally Daddy would have these dreams. War must be terrible, I concluded, if it can make a strong man scream like that.

I was unaware, on that morning that I was taken out to see the "sign," that the Spanish Civil War was setting into motion totalitarian wheels that threatened to crush and destroy the ideals on which civilization had been built.

Hitler came on the scene in my early high school days, and his madness was so evident that we couldn't imagine why he was being followed. What evil charisma drew people to him and made them abdicate their better selves to his devious plans? My father, having met the "enemy" on a previous occasion, thought Germans could only be happy when fighting. I thought of people as individuals, not masses; and I could not believe they all stepped to the same drummer.

I was a junior in high school when the war became a reality. On a bright Sunday afternoon, in the midst of a fellowship dinner in the church basement, Dad brought us the news of Pearl Harbor. Monday was dismal indeed. The idealism back of "the war fought to end all wars" had been a myth. At 11:00 a.m. Franklin Delano Roosevelt declared our nation to be in a state of war. Radios were ready in our classrooms. I was sitting in biology at a lab table, faint odors of formaldehyde drifting around me, when the President's voice, edged with authority, filled the room. At the end of the solemn broadcast we all stood while the strains of our national anthem surrounded us. The strangeness of reality seeped into our bones; the formaldehyde suggested the odor of death. Four boys in the room were doomed at that moment.

I felt schizophrenic about the progress of the war. Sometimes I would avidly follow the news on both fronts; then, satiated with violence, I would not allow myself to look at a newspaper or listen to newscasts for weeks. But curiosity pulled me back.

I started to college in the midst of war. The boys were gone, the news was grim, and my lofty ideas about men and nations were undergoing radical changes.

News began to filter into this country about the "final solution," although it wasn't called that then. Places like Auschwitz, Treblinka, Oblensk slowly became part of our conscious thought. Hitler's *"Nacht und Negel"* plan—night and fog—came to light. It was a simple conception, to move these people into the night and see that they were swallowed up in the foggy mists of his madness, never to be heard from again. Little by little the documents and reports and numbers came through. The disarming statistics were unfathomable—five to six million Jews were tortured, gassed, shot, experimented upon. The sick, the old, pregnant women—all done away with, cruelly and insanely, to satisfy the need for the "final solution."

The term, as some historians suggest, had a mathematical quality about it. Did that help to reduce the human quotient to an abstract dimension? With what kind of psychological protection would one have to be armed to so meticulously carry out such wicked orders?

I pondered these things painfully and quietly. So people were not getting better and better. Maybe my father was right about the Germans, at least half right. Goethe, himself, gone long before the appearance of the Third Reich, said, "I have often felt a bitter sorrow at the thought of the German people, which is so estimable in the individual and so wretched in the generality."

From afar I witnessed through papers and magazines the calculated butchery of human life and human spirit. The question of evil taunted me. If my God, whom I worshiped with devotion, was a God of love, and if he was omnipotent and omniscient, why did he let this happen? If he was not omnipotent, was he God? Wiser and older heads than the one I was equipped with in my nineteenth year had wrestled with that one. Perfidy exists, even in Camelot. It was all very sad. I wanted light and love and peace. I was confronted with darkness, hate, and war.

By the spring of 1945, VE Day was an accomplished fact. Hitler was dead. The Thousand Year Reich had been cut down in its brutal infancy. But the Japanese War continued relentlessly. I spent that summer in Estes Park, Colorado, as a cashier in the famous inn at the National Y Camp. I received cash from notables and less notables, from wealthy refugees who had come out of Austria and found the Rocky Mountains to be a little like home. I wanted to talk to them, but the pain in their faces was fresh, and in their eyes lay a heaviness that I could not trespass against.

Aside from these personal contacts, I forgot the war. I did my job, read, and climbed mountains. On a high peak in the Rockies where the air was thin and the sky a brilliant blue I had a mystical experience. One could be one with God; experience informed me of what I already knew. I was ready to go home.

On August 7, 1945, I ran breathlessly through the Union Station at Denver to the waiting train. By the time I found my seat and got rid of my bags, we were out of the city. I sank into my seat, thankfully. I had made it. Having spent an informal summer in a rustic cabin, I dressed informally for the trip. I was in blue jeans—a little heavier than at the beginning of the summer. The thin air had done something to my appetite. I had eaten six to ten pancakes every morning for a starter. My cheeks were tan and rosy, my hair bleached almost white from the sun. Sitting across from me a comely soldier let me get my breath, and then said, "You are the healthiest looking human being I have ever seen." I thanked him for the most doubtful compliment I had ever received.

Later on he said, "I guess you know about the bomb." "The bomb?" I was puzzled.

"Don't you know the Japanese have had it? We

dropped an atom bomb on a city called Hiroshima. We've won the war!"

I was still puzzled. Atom bombs were something out of science fiction.

"You know," he said, "atomic fission—busting of molecules, that's what it is. Set the whole city ablaze. Thousands were killed. They've had it now; they've got to surrender."

I was trying to absorb it. "They said you could see the flash for miles, it was so bright." I was facing west, the sun was shining in my face with an intensity that was uncomfortable. I tried to imagine the bright flash of the bomb.

The soldier went on. "It must have been a pretty bad thing. People jumped into the river for safety, but the heat from the bomb had made the water boil. Wow!"

The grisly recital of facts turned on my tear ducts, and against my strongest wishes the tears slid down my healthy cheeks.

"Hey, I didn't mean to make you cry. We're winning! We're winning! That should make you happy."

It was a long train ride. Visions of suffering kept me from sleeping. We had dropped the bomb. We, the saviors of the world, had resorted to this. My illusions about a peaceful world vanished.

In a pearly pink dawn I rolled into Iowa and the comforting familiarity acted as a restorative. I arrived home very early. My folks weren't expecting me, so I walked through the deserted town to surprise them. The streets were a rubble of confetti and other souvenirs of victory.

I walked into my parents' bedroom. Dad's first

comment was, "What are you trying to do—get a spot on the Notre Dame team?" Another salute to my state of health. "You've had a good summer, haven't you, dear?" Mother said.

I nodded. Then I said, "I didn't know about the bomb or Hiroshima until I got on the train. This soldier told me."

"Oh, honey!" Mother said. I sat on the edge of the bed and cried. But what could parents say to one who had to face reality sometime? In a sense I had finally come of age.

It was interesting to me that my generation had such a difficult time in dealing with the radical movement of the late 60s and early 70s. It was not as if we had not confronted our own horror both in Hitler's final solution and in the dropping of the A-bomb. Those things happened when we still had a shred of idealism to hang on to. I looked upon those horrifying incidents as a sort of final disillusionment.

These deep feelings of pity and revulsion that I experienced as a college student helped me to bridge the gap with the next generation. Everybody has the right to think things can somehow be made better. So it was without difficulty that I could feel into the helplessness expressed by youth during those tense days of the Vietnam War.

Another experience that helped me to be more realistic, a second coming of age, occurred one summer later when I reached out for something to do that would be in keeping with my major study, sociology.

I ended up out on the western plains of Kansas in a girls' correctional institution in charge of physical recreation. The whole summer's experience had a great impact on me because it was the first time in my life that I truly underwent culture shock. Because my travel experiences had been practically nil, I had had no opportunity really to relate to any culture except that small little corner of the world of which I've already written. Most of the people I'd met were more like me than not, so it was with some trepidation that I made the trip to what was virtually a girls' prison.

About 120 girls were there that summer, about half of them black. There was a great gap in the campus where the administration building had been. The girls had rioted and burned it down a few months before I arrived late on a Saturday evening. My first contact with my summer charges was in their Sunday morning church service. The girls in the choir looked angelic and the girls in the congregation were subdued. It was a false impression that began to right itself in a few hours, and never again would I mistake a choir robe for the robe of an angel.

In classes in criminology I had learned that it was more difficult to incarcerate women than men; consequently, by the time women or girls were in a correctional institution they had been on their way a great deal longer than men or boys. Most of these girls, who ranged in age from about 14 to 21, were there for thievery, prostitution, and, in a few cases, murder. They had had many run-ins with law enforcement agencies before they were actually locked up.

The first thing the gruff superintendent did was to give me a ring with a huge number of keys on it. I had to lock myself in and out of rooms and buildings. It seemed that every few steps I took I had to stop and lock or unlock a door.

She warned me that the girls would "steal me blind," and thus all my possessions were to be locked up in closets and drawers at all times.

The illusions I had arrived with, such as "there is no such thing as a bad girl," were stripped away from me in a hurry. I soon had to accept the fact that there were bad girls. One had to consider—with some compassion—the grim forces of poverty—ghetto life—lack of education—and a deprivation of a value system that made them that way.

One of the problems that occurs among the help in institutions of this type is the fact that people who make this their lifework really do get hardened. They are rare individuals who do not succumb to the hardening process if they have stayed in these institutions too long. When that happens they are no longer able to relate successfully with the people over whom they have so much power. Demoralization then becomes the order of the day, and the whole prison system is trapped in a vicious cycle. It was quite an accepted fact there that, once a girl started down the road that led to this kind of a correctional institution, her entire life would be mostly spent in a prison culture.

I did not have a lot going for me that summer. I was twenty years old, I had finished my junior year at college, and that was my entire portfolio. But I was not hardened, and I could be in a relational capacity to these girls whose years had been spent coping with tragedy in one form or another.

So, even though I knew they were not angels, knew they would steal from me and anyone else available, knew they would go to devious ends for whatever they wanted, I still found much in them to admire. I admired the gusto with which they laughed and played and the resilience with which they warded off, both physically and mentally, hard knocks that would have floored me. I admired the shreds of dignity and self to which they hung tenaciously in spite of the harrowing experiences most of them had had.

They sensed this feeling from me, and I had a significant summer there, working as hard as I could in relating to them in a very personal way. Older, more hardened, and wiser staff members resented my using relationship as a way to make my program go. They assured me daily that I would be sorry, with dire warnings that by opening the door a crack I would let in hordes of problems.

If that happened, I wasn't aware of it. The schoolteacher there never talked face to face with the girls. Everything she wished to impart to them was written on the board in a minute script that was trying even for those with superb vision. The choir director gave most of her signals to them by snapping her fingers. The art teacher taught only occasionally as she was an alcoholic; but in fairness I must say that when she was able to teach, she brought a relational quality to her work.

I left there that summer with a deep appreciation for the deviants among our young people who have lived in such a culture-value vacuum that prison is what we could have predicted for them. I left with a deep sense of appreciation for having been given nurturing parents who could undergird me with a value system that worked out. The first sentence in my criminology textbook made sense: "There, but for the grace of God, go I."

SECOND PERSON

When Great-aunt Mae Albright walked into the drugstore where I found employment following graduation from high school, she was in a hurry as usual. She came bustling up to my cash register and said, "Patty, you can go to college. Your Mother and Dad know all about the arrangements." Dad later told me the interesting story about Aunt Mae giving her farm to McPherson College. As they were closing the arrangement Aunt Mae said to the president, "There's just one stipulation to this. I want my niece to go to McPherson on the income from the farm."

"Well, Mae," replied the president, "We aren't used to doing that."

"And I'm not used to giving away my farms," Aunt Mae retorted quickly. So the matter was settled.

I was elated. Of course, in my fairyland world, I would naturally go to college. It never occurred to me I might not go, but Aunt Mae's reassuring presence and her generous spirit made the dream come true. In her selfless invitation the destiny of my life was secured forever to the Brethren in ways which I could not have dreamed of then.

One early fall evening at McPherson I stopped on the steps that went into the lower level where we all ate together family style, struck by the figure of an obvious newcomer. His back was to me, but the breadth of his shoulders was so inspiring to a sophomore that I could only hope the front view was as impressive as the rear view.

The psychologists inform us that a girl must get her concept of masculinity from her father, and in that short space of time that I held up hungry traffic while I stared at the stranger's back, I remembered my father's shoulders—how immense they seemed to me—how he would come home from a hard day's work and I would watch him as he drank the iced tea Mother had ready for him. His shirt clung to his back, the sweat making dark patches against him, the muscles of his arms strained against his sleeves. I felt comforted by this unconscious display of strength.

An inner awareness informed me that this moment was memorable, that in the brief second that I surveyed bone and body, the direction of my own life was altered.

Blair came to McPherson College in the fall of 1944 from our seminary in Chicago. The small Brethren congregation in Newton, Kansas, needed a pastor, and, because of Newton's proximity to McPherson, it was possible for Blair to complete his undergraduate education there.

On the first Sunday evening of the college year the McPherson church entertained the students at a reception. I was in the midst of my own group of friends. We were notorious for dominating social events with our laughter and noise and with what, we were sure, was witty and sophisticated conversation—when I spotted Blair and found the front view as impressive as the back. He was alone, sitting away from the larger group, perched on the corner of a table.

I observed him a few moments, long enough to reinforce the original impressions of strength. There was force even in immobility—the strapping shoulders, the set of his head—and some inner potency that was a wedding of intelligence and kindness emanated from his blue eyes.

A strange aloofness sent forth signals, something that conveyed the impression that he was alone by preference. Ignoring the signals, I made my way through the crowd and approached him, trying not to betray the fluttering in the depths of my stomach.

"You look too much alone to be in the midst of a party. Won't you come and join us?"

He looked surprised for a moment but quickly hid any feeling under the gallant acceptance, and I took him back to the group, eager to impress him with our collective cleverness.

Much later on, recalling that night, he said he had an impression of being carted off by a very fast young lady. Through all our years of marriage he continues to misjudge my character—and alternates between surprise and pleasure and sometimes disbelief at his union with an atypical Brethren.

Blair came to be known as the "mystery man" the first few weeks he was on campus. Everyone knew some little thing about him, but no one knew much. He was the kind of person who unwittingly generated curiosity in those around him. His aloofness, his quietness, his unwillingness to talk about himself only made us more eager to know more about the stranger.

On a euphoric September evening when the cottonwoods were sending down little fluffs of seedlings and the campus lay in a quiet afterglow of a Kansas sunset, a group of us girls were chattering away in a dorm room that overlooked the main walk of our campus. Someone spotted Blair coming across the campus and said, "There he comes," and we all knew who "he" was.

"Gee," my friend sighed, "I wish we could find out something about him."

Quick as a flash, I headed for the door. "When I return," I said with jesting confidence, "Blair Helman will no longer be a mystery man."

I went down the hall, echoes of derisive laughter following me. As I left the dorm, I looked up to see the surprised faces of my friends, waiting to see just how nervy Pat could be.

An unaesthetic but beloved drinking fountain stood at the apex of our campus. It grieves me now to think that this symbol of Blair's and my first real confrontation has gone the way of the bulldozer and campus planning committee. Blair had unwittingly stopped for a drink, and when he raised up I was there in all my sophomoric glory.

"Hi, Blair!" I projected a feeling of having met a long-lost friend, but his "hello" was edged with surprise again.

With typical Kennedy forthrightness I captivated him with interrogation.

How old was he?

What brought him to McPherson?

How many in his family?

Where was he from?

Was it true he was a coal miner?

How long?

What were his hopes and aims?

How long had he been at Bethany?

Any other work?

There were other questions—I asked them rapidly, and he seemed obliged to be cooperative and to answer me. His basic gentlemanliness kept him from sending me on my errant way with the admonition to mind my own business.

I rushed back to the dorm where the girls were waiting and challenged them to ask me anything about "the mystery man." I quite amazed them with my ample supply of knowledge, but I wondered if I might have paid a high price for a little glory.

Having determined to chastise myself for being so brash, I purposefully left Blair alone. But the process of alphabetical arrangements saved me—on my first day of chemistry lab I discovered my lab partner to be Blair.

The chem lab experience was sort of a capsule of the entire relationship that has existed between Blair and me. He was intent on learning; I was intent on having fun. He brought with him a disciplined mind, a sound knowledge; I brought a quick wit and a woman's intuition. He was fearless; I assumed that place would blow up. He was orderly; I created chaos in a matter of minutes. He was involved in what he was doing; I was involved in what everyone else was doing.

After several bad days when I consumed most of the time asking innocuous questions, very few of them related to the pursuit of knowledge, he led me into a gentlemen's agreement designed to preserve his sanity.

He would work out the problems if I would take care of the equipment. I pretended he was a brilliant scientist and I was his assistant, laying out the test tubes and measuring chemicals. Who would want to bother with formulas when they could observe a noble man at work? Obviously, my feminist leanings hadn't surfaced yet.

Even with his precaution, my presence in the lab took its toll. After many minor skirmishes I dealt Blair the final blow when I forgot to turn the screw clamp on a piece of rubber tubing, and he accidentally got a mouthful of hydrochloric acid. After this horrifying incident, our dear and patient Professor Berkebile suggested I take botany instead of chemistry; so I left by invitation to go to a less dangerous field of endeavor.

This was the beginning of "Pat and Blair," a name-phrase which was to be used oftener and oftener at McPherson.

In the beginning we established a guarded relationship: how much could we hope for from each other, how much could we reveal to each other about the way we really felt? How much safer was a honing of wits—a sort of perpetual battle of the sexes—but always underneath the facade of fun and gaiety, the busyness, was the quiet knowledge that we would be together.

By the time outer plans had caught up with inner certainty I had graduated from McPherson and Blair had received his master's degree at Kansas University along with election to Phi Beta Kappa.

There was the wedding. Since we were far away from Blair's family and our many mutual friends in

Kansas, we deliberately planned a small home wedding to be followed by a large reception so that my clan and family friends could meet Blair.

I came down the staircase into our beautifully decorated living room, on the arm of my father, to Blair who was waiting in front of the fireplace that had been transformed into an altar. Something in the simplicity of the ceremony and the intimacy of the group gathered to witness it literally charged the room with love. By the time the simple words—so laden with responsibility—had been spoken, the entire company had broken into tears, a portentious beginning for the bride and groom.

There was the small parish at Ottawa, Kansas, and a teaching post at Ottawa University. Our first experience together was a wedding of commitment to the soul and the mind. It was prophetic in the sense that Blair's adult life was to be spent in serving Christ through the academic community. Every small experience was a forerunner of the larger but similar experience.

There were struggles and conflicts that surprised the newlyweds. The struggle was mainly of a financial nature—but marriages are compensated by a special bliss in the early years, so that lack of money is a challenge instead of a threat. The conflicts stemmed from the tremendous differences in our temperaments. The "winter and summer" philosophy of getting to know each other contains the basic truth. You learn by trial and error at what point the considerate husband turns into a patriarchal male and at what point the sweet docile bride gets a little shrewish.

It took a few months for the first early rapture to

clear enough for me to see that I had married the last of the great patriarchs. If Blair seemed patriarchal to me, I seemed childish to him. He said I was the only person he knew who would go directly from childhood into senility. Not a very comforting thought when you are feeling mature and even a little sophisticated. Whatever comfort we had together was always in slight disarray because of our perennial battle of the sexes. Blair's ideas about a woman's role and mine were not beautifully synchronized. His own background had prepared him for rather rigid sex roles. My mother had been a career woman, and, while she ran an efficient home, she was always a little beyond a narrow definition of what a female should be. Blair and I have changed a great deal in our perceptions about this question, but we still can engender some heated arguments over the issue.

Whatever the intellectual argument was, nothing was quite as exciting as when I knew I was to become a mother. The experience of bringing life into the world minimizes all other experiences. The whole gamut of creativity, responsibility, and gratefulness for life filled us with awe. Blair carried Bunny into our home—he was a cariacature of the proud father. He beamed—he bragged—he strutted—he planned her life—chose her college and husband while she was still on Simalac. One of our college professors stopped by to take care of the amenities. On observing Blair, she remarked, "A baby can reduce the most rational man to an utter fool."

I had a doll's bed ready for Bunny's first crib. After the baby was situated we sat in silence—complete silence—for over an hour, staring into the crib, watching the little bundle of protoplasm, so perfect, so beautiful, so tiny. We were overcome with the mystery of creation, of life and love. That hour of drinking in the mystical dimension of this new life that was ours, and yet not ours, is one of my most treasured memories of our life together.

THE BEGINNING OF CHANGE

We moved from a small, rural-dominated fellowship into a large city ministry when we went from Ottawa to Wichita, Kansas, in 1954. Ottawa had made a permanent home in our hearts. Our marriage had begun there. We learned of the deep needs in the lives of people we served, and we sensed that wherever we were, some experience in our early years at Ottawa would be seen over and over again—wearing different clothes and speaking a different language. We had come to love the people; we had sat with them in hours of grief, rejoiced with them in small victories of love, and probed with them in an ever deepening spiritual quest.

And, of course, Ottawa would always be that special place because both our daughters had been born there. Four and a half years after Bunny's appearance, Dawn had burst into life with an intensity that belies description. Her presence added more light and love and much laughter to the charmed circle.

We left Ottawa reluctantly, yet we were caught up by an eagerness to meet new people and the challenges afforded to us by change. We enjoyed the life in our new parish—the special sense of belonging that accrues to the minister and his wife when all is well.

The city of Wichita was an exciting place to be. There were concerts to attend, art exhibits to see, an array of good movies from which to choose, and a metropolitan climate that was invigorating.

There was the special time of new friends, and for me there was the challenge of getting back into teaching. The only negative aspect of my working was that I had to leave home base, and accomodations had to be made for my absence.

In spite of those frustrations I felt stimulated by my junior highers. I had a gifted group of children in a brand-new junior high school; together we experienced some really high moments in the classroom.

It is difficult to assess our time in Wichita. We were just moving out of the honeymoon stage with our congregation when developments in another arena promised to bring drastic change to our lives.

One day Blair had gone off with some members of the church board to buy new furniture for his redecorated offices. I was in my usual early afternoon pattern of drinking coffee and chatting with a neighbor when the phone rang. It was a long-distance call from somewhere in Indiana, and I explained Blair's absence. Later in the day another call came, this time from Ohio. My bones began to whisper to me—Manchester College was in the process of finding a president. I explained to my bones that Blair was too young—only thirty-four—with not quite enough experience. The Ph.D. not quite—almost, but not quite—finished. He was at the thesis stage, but a thesis can be formidable. "Hush," I said to my bones and waited for Blair. "He could do it," they answered. "I know!"

Blair didn't come home until after midnight. I had

suggested when Mr. X called the third time that Blair would await his call the following morning. Blair went to his office and told me he would come back to the house as soon as he heard from my gentleman friend, and then he would inform me how wrong my notions were.

After several eons passed, he returned. "They want me to hold an evangelistic service in Ohio," he said a little sadly. "You are not a great evangelist," I said, "but you'd make a great college president. Now tell me the truth."

The truth was that the call was from the chairman of the board of trustees of Manchester College. It set in motion a chain of events that included exciting days, shrouded in secrecy, while decisions were made, appointments kept, and the trustees looked at their candidate. We traveled to Chicago and met the committee of five who had the responsibility of recommending a candidate to the board of trustees. In my berth on the train I lay awake, reflecting on the series of events that led us to this place. Knowing that my presence there meant that they would be passing judgment on me as a person, I prayed that I would do the right thing by this man I loved. Having a reputation for coming forth with startling *faux pas* at critical moments, I prayed for wisdom sufficient to help me be very quiet.

The four-hour interview proved to be very pleasant. Blair discussed education knowledgeably. His years as a professor and his service as chairman of the board of trustees at McPherson College had bred in him a certain authority that was inescapable. I sat very straight and very still. I maintained my nonchalance while keeping my skirt over my knees and my ankles crossed. After a couple hours of erudite conversation from Blair, and a mummy-like countenance from me, one of the men said, "It has occurred to me that Mrs. Helman has sat here for two hours without saying a word. That must be some kind of a record for a woman." I smiled sweetly and didn't indulge the fact that it was indeed a record for me. Another gentleman turned to me and said, "How would you like to be a college president's wife?" Without hesitating I said, "I like being Blair's wife. If he chooses to be a college president, then I'll pour tea, shake hands, or do what I'm called on to do."

At the end of the interview, Blair said, "You folks have been asking me a lot of questions. May I ask you how you came to call me?"

It was an interesting story. Dr. Vernon F. Schwalm, at the end of a fifteen-year tenure at Manchester and a twenty-nine year stretch as college president, announced his retirement in September, effective for the following August. The committee members who shouldered the responsibility of choosing a successor were aware of the magnitude of their job. They sought advice and help from many sources and asked for names of possible choices to be submitted.

At their first meeting, with a list of over one hundred names, they settled into the task of picking several possibilities. They assumed it would take some time to reach consensus on even a few names because of the democratic approach they were using. They decided to express their choices by written ballot and to reach agreement by a process of elimination.

Blair was not personally known to any of the five—none of them had met him, none of them knew what he looked like. In the western region of our church he was well known but not in the central area.

The first ballots were passed out. The chairman said he would write their various choices on a blackboard and they would continue. Amazingly, all five persons—on the first ballot—had voted on some strange young man out in Kansas they really knew nothing about. There was a moment of hushed silence when Blair's name was written on the board for the fifth time.

A dear brother broke the silence by saying, "We have been led. I only see this as the will of God." It was a touching story, and Blair and I both felt humble as they told us.

Before we left Chicago's Palmer House we were informed that they would recommend to the entire board that Blair be Manchester's new president. At the proper time, by a unanimous vote, Blair was called to the most challenging experience of his life.

On the train going back to Wichita, we were like two excited little children. We had a huge and delicious secret that we must hug to ourselves for several weeks. Dreams were being realized—dreams that had allayed some of the frustration and bitter work of the coal mines, dreams that had filled a poor little boy's head as he bent over his books in the circle of light made by the coal oil lamp. And now new dreams took over. What kind of life was ahead of us, what exciting days and years had been given to us at the Palmer House?

Back in Wichita, lying in bed and pondering over the new life we had chosen, Blair said to me, "You realize, Pat, we've reached the point of no return. The commitment is total!" I thought I understood then what he was saying. But the years have brought a depth of understanding that comes only with experience.

FAMILY AFFAIR

I decided, very late on the night of July 31, 1956, that North Manchester, Indiana did not exist. We had traveled for hours and hours, having left Kansas at sunset twenty-four hours previous, and having had only a short break for rest.

Dawn and Bunny were suffering from travel fatigue, which meant that hysteria replaced sleep. They were either fighting or giggling; and one of my first acts on entering the state of Indiana was to grab a road map and flail it around, hoping to connect with either bundle of irritation in the back seat. My own travel fatigue was getting the best of me when I finally spotted a sign—North Manchester, 10 miles. Finally we arrived—travel-worn and weary. David Yeatter, the treasurer of the college, met us and situated us for the night; his wife, Mary, furnishing us with clean sheets. We were placed in the college health center until our home would be ready.

Blair's new work would begin the next morning, and we looked at those beds as a thirsting man looks at clear, cool water. I was awakened early by an enterprising milkman who wanted to sign me up for a lifetime milk supply. I signed and fell back into bed. The doorbell rang—my caller wanted me to subscribe to the college newspaper. Were there to be no fringe benefits?

Blair informed me we were to be guests at a luncheon, to have the girls ready, et cetera. I looked at my sleeping darlings and knew they would disgrace me before 2:00 p.m.

The doorbell rang. An old, old man was standing there. "Are you the new president's wife?" he asked. I assured him I was. He peered through the screen. "Could you step outside a minute?" I obeyed. He peered into my face. "Just wanted to look at you," he said and walked away, shaking his head. I was already a failure.

That first day of welcomings, of doorbell ringings, of handshakings, was evidence of much that was ahead. In the months following we received a warm reception from many people. The academic community has its own style. Our new friends were stimulating, the social life interesting if exhausting, and whole vistas of a new life opened before us. We moved into a large house that soon was our home, and we started adjusting. An observer would assume that we had it made. Everything looked great—everything sounded great.

In November of 1956 Blair's inauguration took place with all the attendant pomp and ceremony. I suppose it was quite a normal reaction for my heart to be filled with pride as I saw a huge audience of strangers—erudite strangers—and friends and family stand to do honor to Blair. In the midst of the crowd I recall experiencing a lonely feeling, a feeling that I and I alone knew what a hard road it had been that had led to this place. The responsibility he had assumed at Manchester was spelled out clearly by the various ones who had charge of the inauguration.

As I look back on that day in retrospect, it is vague, hazy, and assumes in a dream-like quality. There would be some advantage in having more time to get acquainted—to feel one's way with more surety than we had by the time this event occurred. Whatever personal shortcomings we may have felt, the day was exciting and had all the qualities that Abraham Maslow demands for a "peak experience."

On the home front there was a subtle but certain shift in family pattern and relationship—I had a rival. I felt something moving out ahead of me. I was no longer the center of Blair's life. I was shoved a little to the left or right, but I was not the center.

Manchester College became the center. Bricks and timbers and strangers, committee meetings, correspondence, travel, speeches—the whole gamut of administration absorbed Blair—absorbed him entirely.

And I felt very sorry for myself. In our years together Blair and I had seldom been separated. As a pastor he had an office next door to the house, and we had an inter-phone system—we could be in touch at the flick of a switch. Blair's work involved me. When he made pastoral calls, he desired me to accompany him. Our social life was entwined with the social life of the church. When he was in the pulpit, I was in the pew. We understood, believed in, and practiced togetherness. We functioned as units of two and four—never one and three.

So I was not prepared for the sudden separation, both in body and spirit, that seemed to be taking place.

Blair disappeared early in the morning into a hard world which he cultivated assiduously because he did have a great deal to learn.

I missed him—I missed his company and I missed the total involvement in his work that I had always known. To be sure, I was busy—I did pour tea, and entertain, and sit at the speaker's table—but I felt more ornamental than useful.

I began to be angry—it was a deep anger hidden beneath a ready smile and a lot of activity. So this was the point of no return, the total commitment he had spoken of so long before in Wichita.

I was angry on behalf of Dawn and Bunny. They missed their dad. They reminded me of the picnics we had in Ottawa and Wichita, of afternoons at the zoo, of early evenings at Kiddie Land. I didn't hide my resentment. I shared it with them.

And they were frightened that something would happen to him. One night when Blair was due in on a plane, it was storming very hard. Dawn was sitting in a big chair, huddled under a blanket. Bunny and I were discussing whether or not the storm would delay Blair's flight. Suddenly Dawn shouted with six-year-old vehemence, "You be quiet! You should know by now I'm praying for Daddy."

The pace was telling on Blair. He became crabby— and the precious time when he was with us was eaten up in bickering. And I, nursing my hurt, always had to come back. If he wanted trouble, I would be glad to oblige.

For the first time in our married lives we were not living at that joyous level we had set for ourselves. I felt burdened, with nowhere to turn. The fact that on the surface our lives must seem impeccable only added to my anger.

Whenever I'm low, I have little conversations with myself—two levels of being argue back and forth, searching for answers.

"What's wrong with you? You didn't used to carry on like that."

"I'm mad—hurt—angry."

"What do you want?"

"I want to go back before the point of no return."

"Can't."

"I know."

"Anyway—where's that joy, joy, joy you talk about?"

"Gone—maybe forever."

"You are low."

"But I still believe."

"Ya—you look like it—a real loving believer."

"I am loving."

"Who are you trying to convince?"

"Me!"

I am aware, in retrospect, that whenever my need has been particularly great an answer comes. It may be years before I recognize that a particular person or situation is an answer, but the pattern evolves.

At that particular low point in our marital experience, and in my spiritual life, an answer came. It didn't look like an answer. It was only a small book—the life of an obscure woman, Florence Allshorn, who had founded a community on the basis of the two great commandments. The dear friend who sent it to me wrote a note in which she stated that she thought Allshorn would be of interest to me. She wasn't sure why, except that as she read the book she kept thinking of me.

I perused the book without any great interest, but suddenly the words grabbed me. They seemed illuminated, full of light, written to me, for me. Suddenly all the mistakes of my "period of adjustment" became so clear.

The biggest mistake I was making was the most human mistake of all. I was being very selfish. I was trying to hold onto something that was in the past, something that had been satisfying but was no longer possible.

Another experience I had about the same time put my dilemma even more sharply into focus. Blair was sensitive to what was happening. He tried, albeit often unsuccessfully, to get time for us to be together so the communication channels could stay open. For about a week I had looked forward to this particular Wednesday night when just the two of us were to go to a nearby city for dinner and a show.

When Blair came home, he explained that at least part of our plans would have to be changed. There was a dispossessed Latvian family in town whose son was in college. He passed our home on the way to the campus, a tall handsome young man; and I knew the family of whom Blair was speaking. I did not know the mother had died, and Blair said we must go to the funeral home and visit the family. We would still have time for dinner but not for the show.

I was angry, and I said so. Perhaps we could make the funeral-home stop another time. That was out of the question. My anger escalated. How come it always happened that events outside our influence kept us from doing what we personally wanted to do? I went on and on but eventually found myself at the door of the funeral home.

The young bereaved Latvian seemed very touched that we had come to pay our respects to his mother. I stood by the coffin, and I saw there a regally beautiful woman—serene in death, her white hair piled on top of her white head. In her hands was a spray of three roses, and she was wearing a beautiful signet ring.

Our student friend talked at length about his mother—how she had lost everything in the war, including two sons, her first husband, her father, and then her second husband. In Latvia she had been highly respected as one of the leading child educators of the little country. But in America almost no one knew of her great capabilities. Here she had cleaned houses for people, but she was grateful for life and for the opportunity for her only remaining son to get an education.

I left the funeral home feeling very small and petty. I had not known grief through such desolate kinds of loss. I had never been wrenched away from the place I loved or been shorn of my credentials.

Things suddenly fell into place. I had been living selfishly, and the selfishness blinded me to what I had been doing to those closest to me. I began to get things turned around in my head and heart. I became more self-aware than ever, because I had to watch and control the enemy within.

Florence Allshorn said that the only way we could authentically reflect the nature of Christ was to come completely out of ourselves—to be able to serve in whatever station we found ourselves. My station was 714 Bond Street. Never had Blair needed me more than he did now. He needed love and trust and help—not whining and bickering. The book, together with the experience at the funeral home, opened eyes that had been blinded by selfishness. Little by little the healing process began. Little by little, as I took myself out of the center of my existence, the bright light of joy returned.

We learned to live with a job that demands one's whole self. Not overnight, but gradually, I learned, and I helped the girls to accept this blunt fact. The work is of first consideration. One must make choices in light of how the college is best served. One's own desire for fun, for time together, for anonymity, gives way to the call. The balancing factor that paid off for the lonely nights, the changed relationships, and the physical exhaustion is what hard-headed economists refer to as psychic income.

Part of the psychic income came by way of interesting personalities who crossed our threshold. My first dinner guest of renown was Eleanor Roosevelt. I was just naive enough to prepare and serve the meal myself—remembering her healthy appetite, I concluded that it suited her. Frank Laubach gave Dawn her first reading lesson, and Ogden Nash recited poetry for the girls.

Martin Luther King stood before us a completely free man yet paradoxically a slave to a cause that has already changed the lives of thousands of people. The presence of Roy Burkhart, founder of famous Community Church in Columbus, Ohio, was a joy because of his contagious spirit of love.

During Dr. Burkhart's stay here, Dawn and Bunny had indulged in a sisterly fight. Dawn, laboring under a remorseful spirit, wrote Bunny a note that said, "I love you, Bunny. Your sister" and taped it to the bathroom mirror. When he saw it, Dr. Burkhart wrote on a bigger piece of paper, "I love you both. Roy Burkhart" and taped it beside the smaller one.

There is a certain quality in persons whose lives have affected many others that makes this kind of experience a gift. The list includes the great and near-great from the world of politics, the arts, government—the gamut of our national life.

There are many evidences of added benefits, but it is never so clear as on Commencement Day when Blair hands out diplomas to several hundred young men and women who are going out to serve in a variety of ways—teachers, doctors, ministers, lawyers. Then I know again that it is all worth it.

The years in North Manchester have been characterized by growth—in love, in patience, in the ability to grant one another a certain freedom in thought and action that has allowed each of us to develop in our own style. We have tried to give this freedom to Bunny and Dawn, so they will have the joy of finding their own identity.

And for both Blair and me, inherent in our style has been growth in the spirit. We are aware that spiritual values seem to have no decisive influence on the destiny of our culture. This awareness only strengthens our desire to bring to bear, in our own sphere of influence, that vital truth by which we structure our lives.

Aside and apart from our love for each other and family we have a common goal—meeting the demands of commitment to something beyond ourselves—that has added lustre and strength to an enduring marriage.

113

POINT BETSIE INTERLUDE:
ALPHA AND OMEGA

At Point Betsie, clothed in a shimmer of grace that tears the heart with beauty, the morning and evening assume the dimensions of the Alpha and Omega.

One particular Monday morning I recall because Sunday had been a stormy day. The Sabbath stillness had been broken by the constant groan of the fog horn, and waves had broken against the beach and the jetties in front of the lighthouse with an angry white ferociousness. On this particular morning I sat on a dune, high above the lake, and the words of a song came back again and again, "How wonderful the hand of God."

The lake was placid except at the beach where curling fingers of foam grabbed vainly for the rocks—it seemed too tired after its day of tossing and churning to even try very hard. The sky was almost without color, a pale, opaque blue unmarked by any clouds. At the horizon it became deeper, a symmetrical band of blue that surrounded the lake and seemed to cut it off from the sky itself.

In the early morning sun the sand was gold, and the growth that had taken hold of the dunes was first silver, then green and gold, as it turned and swayed with the breeze. As the grasses turned and dipped they made concentric markings in the sand, looking for all the world as if some child had drawn a circle around every clump of dunes grass.

The beach stretched out before me, a mosaic of stone and driftwood. To the north the red roof of the lighthouse lent vivid color to the scene, and to the south the beach ended in a curve that beckoned you to go and see what was beyond.

Birds flew above me, making intricate patterns of curves and arches as they circled and glided along their path. The gulls, now working hard at flying, then taking a long breather, soared against the heavens, teasing their earthbound watchers with their grace and proficiency.

My heart was full of thanks—thanks for the wonderful hand of God that created this world so beautifully, that no matter which way I turned I was confronted with it. And thankful I was for the peace and stillness in the early morning—and for time to open my hungry soul and let the still small voice come to me in the waves, on the beach, in the very air that was filled with God's messengers.

If every night is a foretaste of death, every morning is a reminder of the constant resurrection of life, as God's light bathes the world in brightness. So the dawn had about it a pristine quality, the drama of renewal, of hope, of a pure beginning.

I gathered all the gloriousness of my surroundings into my soul. And it was glory to know that this little area of the universe was still almost untouched by the demands of civilization. It was as God had made it—no bulldozers, no city planning, no beautification com-

116

mittees—just the sand arranged in the proper symmetry, outlined by the deep pine forests, fronted by the expanse of the lake, and lit up with God's own light.

Toward evening the tourists would begin to arrive, cameras in hand, to view and capture the famous Point Betsie sunset. Cars would be lined up for a long way on the lighthouse road, their occupants ready for one of nature's special treats.

Each night the western sky held us by its beauty, whether it was flamboyant or ethereal, vivid or pastel. I am convinced that for beauty in the evening you need wide, unbroken spaces, where the colors have room for range and depth. I remember the sunsets in Kansas, where the distant horizon is broken only by the golden waves of wheat, not unlike the long sweep of horizon on any great body of water.

We roamed the beach and the dunes to find good spots for the unbroken view. Sometimes we sat high on the dunes and looked out over the sandy hills at God's spectacular way of tucking in his children. Other times we sat on the huge twisted logs on the beach and looked westward as a fantastic parade of color changed before our eyes.

One night I recall vividly because the sky had been overcast all day, and I was fearful that the sunset would not be visible. As evening came the sky and lake melted into a vaporous gray that erased the horizon. When it seemed there would be no color to enchant us, a tiny opening appeared behind which the sun blazed in violent glory, edging the small space with gold. From this seemingly small opening a golden path was laid on the still waters that literally seemed to come across the lake right to our feet. All of us were reminded of Jacob's ladder. It seemed that with faith and imagination we could have walked on that golden path, straight into the arms of love.

Another evening the sky was ablaze with the red-gold ball that threw light promiscuously over the whole lake. Above the sun were wispy airy clouds that floated upward, giving the impression of huge angel wings dusting off the stars. And directly above us a huge silvery circle gave promise of a full moon, an enchanting night for young lovers, a tender night for those whose love was burning with the steady glow that only time can give.

For the morning and evenings at Point Betsie we are grateful. For the beginning and ending of all days we give thanks. And in the great Alpha and Omega, even Christ himself, we place our trust that both the beginning and the end, the first and last, are good.

O DAY OF REST AND GLADNESS

If the Sundays I have lived through were to be subtracted from my life, it would be a lesser life. Not just because some time had been removed, but because a certain quality of experience would be gone.

As I give a long look at my life, I realize what a regular, consistent, sustaining foundation the church has been for me. There were those impressionable years when I went about by myself or with my sisters, engaged in a "variety of religious" experiences. There were those years among the Disciples of Christ when their pastor made such an impact on my life. We had communion then every Sunday because the Disciples felt this was to be obedient to the Scriptures, and I believed they had the truth.

As things got better for my family financially, we finally got a car and aligned ourselves with the Brethren once again at the Iowa River church near Marshalltown. There I had the new experience of sitting in a pew with my whole family and a sense that together we were making a real contribution to the church.

Finally, as the wife of a minister, perfect attendance

was exacted of me. In the two parishes Blair served following our marriage—Ottawa and Wichita, Kansas—I felt myself to be at the very heartbeat of the congregation. I enjoyed the role—I rose to the best of my abilities to fulfill other peoples' expectations. It was the kind of sacred soil in which I grew, and those days in the parish fleshed out the life-long quest in which I had been involved.

I have developed a kind of schizophrenia about the organized church. I have sat through church services glassy-eyed, tuning out the irrelevancies falling from the pulpit. At times I have had the distinct impression that the oxygen supply to my brain had been cut off, so disoriented from real life the church seemed to be. In the case of committee meetings, I go buoyantly, only to discover halfway through the meeting that I am drowning in trivia, immersed and rendered senseless by nothingness. I have accepted so many stones in my quest for bread that the "Christian life" sometimes seems more burden than joy. But hidden somewhere in that morass of administration and programming is the spark of vitality. It is Christ himself, whose body the church is, at work in a world that cries to be saved from its brokenness.

And for that spark of vitality I return again and again, for on occasion some perceptive preacher fans it to life, some great music presents it in a blaze of glory. And sometimes God comes to me in that remembered candence of his church. "The kingdom of this world has become the kingdom of our Lord."

My schizophrenia manifests itself in despair when men and women insist on being misguided instead of led by God's word—in joy when I sense the reality of

Christ. My quest continues for wholeness, for a reconciliation between what the church is and what the church can be.

I get angry when I see the church used as an extra service club—a sort of a Sabbath Kiwanis gathering. I get angry when I see men and women in leadership roles in the church so concerned about horizontal relationships that the vertical relationship—that which is happening between God and his creatures— seems so often to be forgotten. I am puzzled when ministers and lay persons alike shy away from a Christ-centered position—especially among Brethren who speak of themselves rather glibly as a New Testament church. For what is the New Testament but a collection of material concerning Christ, whose name we take in vain if we refuse him the central position in our churches and in our lives?

However, in spite of my anger I could not do without the church. As I have lived through violent changes in society and sense the "transvaluation of values" that Nietzche predicted a century ago, I cling to the hope that Christ through his church will be triumphant.

When Blair was pastor of the little church in Ottawa, we were in Kansas City one Sunday on a preaching mission. We were to be back at Ottawa in the evening for our fall communion and love feast, held in the poor little basement that was not too unlike the catacombs.

We left Kansas City later than we expected and, following the advice of well-meaning friends, took a short cut through Olathe to speed our journey home. Suddenly we were caught in indescribable traffic, and we remembered too late the huge yearly air show held at the big Olathe Air Base. Thousands of people were going and coming on the narrow Kansas highway. The cars were bumper to bumper for miles, and the pace was limited to about twenty miles an hour.

We were very tense because of our responsibilities at home, and we were aware of terrific tensions and hostility surrounding us. Drivers were cursing and yelling, horns were honking. Above us fighter planes were screaming and diving. The noise beat against our very spirits.

Finally we got out of the traffic and arrived home—a few minutes late and not really prepared mentally or physically for communion. Breathlessly we dashed into the parsonage and grabbed what we needed, then ran next door to the church and down the basement steps to where our people were waiting.

The candles were flickering against the crude cement walls. Everything was hushed, the people were waiting for us—and the effect was sheer drama. Out of noise and fear and tension we walked into the church at its best. This was the body of Christ, worshipful, patient, loving.

The parishioners sat in an attitude of prayer, the women in their prayer veils, the men strong in their quietness. They had come in from the farms; there were teachers, a postman, a banker, a cabinetmaker, widows, and children—all waiting for the bread of life to be broken unto them. I knew them all well. I knew that the next morning they would be at their various stations and in some way would carry into their spheres of influence the sensitivity of Christ. In conversations with neighbors, in a teacher's relationship to her children, in the postman's rounds, the grace of God would be manifest.

Blair's voice had never had more authority than when he read the Scriptures that night. As I knelt to wash the feet of my sister, tears streamed down my face. How much the world needed some evidence of humility, some evidence of a willingness to be servant instead of master.

That night the eucharist achieved its full meaning—could I be transformed, could Christ live in me? I thought so. As we sang the old hymn that has closed love feasts for generations, my heart was full:

> Blest be the tie that binds
> Our hearts in Christian love.
> The fellowship of kindred minds
> Is like to that above.

We had moved from hell to heaven that evening. We are always bounded by both—and the church does make straight the way.

I need and enjoy the contemplative life, but I can't enjoy that luxury without accepting the attendant responsibility contemplation implies. Jesus Christ walked among men—so the church, as his body, must keep walking, healing, lifting. One reason I give my heart to the Brethren so willingly is that at our best this mission of Christ to be in the world but not of the world is totally relevant to us. We try to move in a secular society, to bring the nature of Christ to bear upon that society. Free as we are to reinterpret the New Testament in the light of new insights, we understand more and more clearly Jesus' admonition: "Inasmuch as you have done it unto the least of these my brethren, you have done it unto me."

So, in spite of my split personality, I shall always go back. I shall always support. No amount of learning or sophistication can turn me away from the church. I shall always turn Bunny and Dawn toward the church and trust it will have deep meaning in their lives.

Sunday after Sunday after Sunday you can find me in my pew. Sometimes I could only be described as a large lump of protoplasm, osmosing bits of sound and sensation. But another time there will be joy ineffable, love inescapable; and I can truly say, "Oh, for a thousand tongues to sing my dear Redeemer's praise."

Thank God for all my Sundays.

TREASURES OF DARKNESS

I read all the words I have written. Is there too much light, too much success, is the family too close, are there no shadows? How wrong it would be to claim only light, for what would light be without darkness to show its brilliance? I confess we have often walked in darkness—sometimes spiritual, but usually physical.

Our Manchester years have been marked with vicissitude. Blair's major coronary and his absence from the office for months is a story in itself. Bunny's and Dawn's polio is another story. My miscarriage opened the book.

All of these situations have thrown us into the shadows. The valley of the shadow is a reality. Over and over again we have experienced what Douglas Steere calls the "Grand Canyon experience" of the soul, where the winds of God sweep through, blowing where they will.

I write about this finally because the tragic experiences of life give perspective, just as the cross gives perspective to our faith. To deny that underlying all our lives is a thread of loss of pain and desolation, seems to me to deny a great part of the human experience. Although the expression of my faith is a

125

reverent joy in life, the fact of my faith has been sharpened and made evidential through the difficult trials of alienation and pain.

It is of some interest to me that preceding every "Grand Canyon experience" of my life, I have felt some precognition, some brooding sense of preparation for what lies ahead. Sometimes it is only in retrospect that one remembers such readiness for the *via dolorosa*; other times one cannot escape the existentialist feeling of the "here and now" sensitivity to the future. One of the most striking of these experiences occurred following Blair's homecoming after a month's hospital stay due to a heart attack.

It was February, a bitter cold day, the ground submerged in deep layers of snow. Blair was resting comfortably and looking forward to resuming his normal activities and work. I had walked to the college to pick up his mail. On my return, as I was crossing the street about a block from home, I was caught, stopped still by some vague sense of uneasiness. I looked down the street toward home and on down as far as I could see, where a curve about four blocks distant cut off my vision.

My heart was cold—the cold had seeped into every bone—chilling me with a sense of fear. As far as I could see, there was no living thing. The black trees spread skeletal fingers against a somber gray sky. No rush of birds' wings broke the silence—no human figure put movement into the still-life that lay before me. Not even a car motor could be heard—nothing to indicate life—just black and white cold and silence that penetrated to my very heart. It was as if I heard a voice say, "You have a long, cold, hard road to walk, and you must walk it alone!"

I hurried home, fully expecting to find Blair in the agonizing throes of another heart attack. He seemed fine. Oh, it was a mistake, I thought. It is over—the long, hard walk. But my mind could not convince my heart. The sense of foreboding hovered over me, stifling my energy, sapping my strength.

The premonition of disaster was so strong that I found myself praying constantly that whatever was ahead, I would be prepared—that spiritual strength might bolster human strength, that I could face whatever came. And it came—more hospitalization, trips to the Mayo Clinic, trips south, searching for answers, the doctor's dire warnings that Blair would never work again. All this lasted for many rugged months, and in spite of love and concern and help that I could not have done without, I felt alone. It was one of the darkest periods of our life. In my aloneness I knew God was there—out of reach for me momentarily—but some steadying faith got me through, and the light broke upon us again.

In retrospect, the whole experience took on a spiritual intensity, enabling us to re-assess our values and reexamine our love for each other. Once more God had demanded a leap of faith. With what joy we acquiesced! Blair's triumph over the physical, his return to work, and the continuing contribution he makes has the dimensions of a miracle.

Some months ago again I sensed the heaviness of heart and spirit that I have begun to recognize as a warning. Like T. S. Eliot, it isn't that I believe in the furies—it's just that I can hear the beating of their wings.

All fall my physical condition bothered me. While nothing seemed obviously wrong, something obviously was wrong. Remembering a period of illness in my mother's life that had been similar, I did a little self-diagnosing and decided I was having gall bladder trouble. I told our beloved family doctor this; and humoring me good naturedly, he sent me for X rays. On the day before Thanksgiving the report came back indicating that I had diagnosed myself correctly. Both the doctor and I agreed that after the holidays were over I would, at some propitious time, make arrangements for surgery.

We made a short trip for Thanksgiving, and on the way home late Thanksgiving night, I said to the family, "I don't think I'll be home for Christmas." This announcement, made in all seriousness, was met with laughter, gentle pats on the back, and such ingenuous phrases as "Buck up, kid!"

To understand the import of this thought in my own mind, you must understand what happens to me at Christmastime. What restraint I might feel in keeping with the Brethren ethic of the simple life escapes me completely as the "happiest and holiest" of seasons descends upon us. For weeks I plan and work, I paint and sculpt, and I cut stained glass, all toward the end of a beautifully decorated home. Hours are spent in the intricate task of jeweling and decorating exquisite eggs that adorn a huge gold tree. Whatever aesthetic talents may be mine are all brought to bear on our Christmas house.

Through the years the collection of decorations has grown along with a certain reputation concerning our home. For me, the whole task has assumed spiritual dimensions. By the time the last touches have been lovingly given and the lights and candles are lit, I feel I've built a small cathedral, an offering befitting a King.

Then begin the teas and small suppers, all the hospitality that takes on an extra dimension of love because of the season. So, knowing what lay ahead—what had become the natural expectation of family and friends—I felt beholden to stay very healthy during my time of the year.

I went to bed Thanksgiving night afflicted with a sense of heaviness, both physical and spiritual. At 5:00 the next morning, I wakened Blair. I was terribly ill and in much pain. The doctor came, and with the tell-tale X rays so available, he said I must go in for surgery.

I cried, out of pain and frustration, and said if I left I knew I wouldn't be home for Christmas. They all pooh-poohed me and said nonsense, and I obediently took the only course opened to me.

There began, then, what was to be my own "forty days and forty nights" in the wilderness—a series of physical traumas that, even in retrospect, is difficult to face.

I was very sick following surgery, but for awhile I made progress. My surgery came shortly after President Johnson's; and Blair regaled me with clever questions like: "Tell me, Pat, would you have felt like running the affairs of state two hours after coming out from the anesthetic?" This was purely academic; he knows better than anyone that I have a difficult time running my own affairs. I tried to be a model patient, I walked painfully up and down the hall, brightened up for visitors, and in all ways intended to be on the "gall bladder schedule."

A week after my surgery, when all things pointed to a normal recovery, Blair had to go to New York. Bunny and Dawn made their regular evening appearance at the hospital; and our friends, aware of Blair's absence, were kindly attentive. when he returned, expecting to take me home, I had to admit I didn't have any obvious symptoms to report, but I knew I was worse instead of better.

An unexplained weakness had seized me, and the thought of expending any effort increased my discomfort. my legs were cold and clammy. the doctors listened patiently. I don't think they believed me. Seven days following the initial surgery, the symptoms became more explicit. I started running a temperature, and the abdominal pain, which had never disappeared, became more and more severe. There followed four grim days as my temperature soared to 104°, and the pain became unbearable without hypos.

For my part, I retreated into the world of illness, becoming almost totally unaware of any exterior happenings. I think the body can be so desperate that one naturally focuses all attention on the process of keeping alive. People came and went—they were only familiar shadows—the mail lay untouched, other offerings of love unseen. I was involved in a struggle with death.

On December 17, after a night spent in the constant company of nurses and doctors, I was taken back to surgery. Two major abdominal surgeries in less than three weeks can lay low even the most valiant spirit. The diagnosis the second time around was chemical peritonitis and other complications. Following that operation, my adrenal glands stopped working, and for some seventy-two hours, I was the despair of the doctors. Hooked up to several medical devices, unconscious of reality, I managed to stay with it. At the proper time they gave me massive doses of cortisone which slowly righted the adrenalin situation.

As I had foreseen, December did not possess the gaiety and sparkle that it has always had for our family. For Bunny and Dawn, this was another crisis that called for endurance at a tender age. While Blair often gives the impression of being a perambulating Rock of Gibraltar, his burdens are always heavy, and I added to them mightily. It was a bleak time indeed.

But we had Christmas, and we knew the joy that is the heart of Christmas. The girls put up a tiny but beautiful tree in my room, the three of them came like the Magi, bearing gifts. By Christmas Day I was thankful to be well enough to communicate with them after two weeks of virtual silence. I was too weak to remove the wrappings from the gifts, but there were willing hands and bright eyes and as much gaiety as one can put into a hospital room. When I felt myself sinking into a really desperate fight for life, I had prayed a strange prayer. I prayed that I would not die at Christmas time, because I knew that would lay a shadow on my family at Christmas that could never be entirely lifted. On that Christmas Day they could not know how filled my heart was with thanksgiving.

One does not live through an experience like this without gaining new insights. I found myself living on two levels. There was the physical level, the pain and weariness and shock, the humiliation that finally sets in when you are needfully treated as being only flesh and bones. But there was another level, that of the spirit. A dear friend reminded me of this verse in Isaiah: "I will give thee the treasures of darkness."

And there were treasures. There was an awareness of God's light and love, of the concern and affection of many friends, the heightened senses of the bonds of family which time and separation do not loosen.

And for days, when I was not consciously responding to the world about me, I was conscious of the spirit.

One of the things I hated to give up was the Christmas music, the college choirs, the carolers, the church programs that lifted me beyond myself in a spirit of adoration. Part of the consciousness of the spirit involved hearing a beautiful choir. There were "Glorias" and "Hallelujahs," all in perfect harmony, that soothed me and insulated me from the harsh hospital sounds. Evidently I asked others if they were enjoying the music, because one of my first conscious memories following the second operation was Blair bending over me and saying, "Honey, don't ask anyone else about the choir. Evidently that is being piped in just to you."

Later the doctors told me I had experienced auditory hallucinations, but by any name the music was a balm and blessing.

Along with the music was a heightened awareness of the terrain of my life. It was as if I were looking over a landscape, back over mountains I had climbed and valleys I had struggled through. The gift of belief had always been a part of my experience; but during those days when I seemed clinically out of it, I was recounting steps in my spiritual growth

The first little mountain was the ability, finally, to face reality, to sense the underlying tragedy of life and adjust my vision to see the truth. When I did this, I realized my God was even greater than I thought. He became the suffering servant, he wept over the city, he walked among men so they could measure the greatness of his love against the bleakness of their own lives.

The second milestone on the spiritual terrain came early in my adult life. At the little church in Ottawa, as the new bride of their much respected young minister, I already had my way partly made. What I had not reckoned with was how much the people might expect of me. They looked to me for many things, and I was grateful that I related easily to them. But I knew I was not equipped to lead in any spiritual way. It was here that I began a search that is still going on. It was a search of the printed page, but the words were written by the saints of the church. I was surprised at how many facts from the Holy Scriptures I could dredge up from my Sunday school days. But I longed for fresh insights, for new direction. Whenever I heard of any literature that seemed to be an authentic expression or source of a relationship with God, I read it. I wanted to be a channel—more than a channel, a reservoir—full and overflowing.

Climbing a little higher, the next insight that brought change was the beginning of an understanding about the nature of Christ's love. It is not enough for me to be knowledgeable, to be well-read, to pray. I must learn to love in his way—not a selfish "I'll love you if you love me" approach. My love must bear some stamp of an authenticity that comes from Christ. I love because you are. And my love cannot be limited to those closest to me, to those like me; authentic Christian love is an embracing emotion that reaches out for all of God's children, that is inclusive yet never fails to be personal, a love that sets all people free from status, color, and condition.

Lying there enmeshed in illness, a prisoner in sterile surroundings, I moved toward greater light. It was a move to surrender—the final acknowledgement that I am not, by any stretch of the imagination, the "master of my own fate." Admittedly, there are days—months, maybe years—when I am. But one cannot escape those moments of reckoning.

There is still physical trauma to be met. As the victim of a strange blood chemistry disease, my familiarity with the hospital sometimes makes it seem like my "home away from home." There is the sudden and painful onslaught of sickness, the strange days of struggle in the hospital, and the aftermath of pain and weakness with which one must contend.

There is also a knowing that personal loss must sometime be faced. With aged parents and other uncertainties bearing in on you, you must begin to be realistic about a sense of personal tragedy.

The sudden twists and turns in life will buffet you like tumbleweed in the canyon, ready or not. How great to be able truly to say with Augustine: "I toss upon the waves, but Thou dost steer. Thou who standest at the helm of all things Thou hast made."

POINT BETSIE INTERLUDE: LUMEN CHRISTI

We are back at Point Betsie. We've come back year after year, drawn there by the mystery and silence and isolation.

I sit on a huge gnarled log, twisted, weathered with sand and water and time into an object of silvery beauty. I watch Blair from my vantage point, a shadowy presence a long way down the beach. Like the log, Blair has weathered well.

The strength that first attracted me is still there; the sense of promise is in the process of fulfillment, the kindness as natural as drawing breath, the intelligence sharpened by experience to a keen bright finish. He is walking toward me and I am reminded of a phrase from some remote reading, "the face is a mirror of indestructible character." That is the essence—out of the fire of back-breaking work and struggle—of discipline and commitment, the indestructible character.

Our relationship has weathered well, too. Love demands care and response and attention. Blair and I have paid attention to each other. Soon thirty years will have passed our marriage by, and someone has suggested that love can be defined as what you've been through together. With a thirty-year perspective, that makes sense.

The girls are running toward us, their hair flying in the wind, their lithe bodies glistening in the sun. They have found some Petoskeys. They laughingly show them to their dad—this puts them ahead of him—the race has just begun.

One summer soon we must come alone. They are growing up, their plans are not always family plans. Now we savor this time together.

The three of them move down the beach. I gaze contentedly around me. I haven't told you about the lighthouse. I must, because it dominates the whole Point Betsie scene.

There it sits, stolidly built upon a point of sandy rise, protected by huge seawalls and massive iron jetties, commanding a complete view of the lake and all its surroundings. Its white bricks gleam in the sunlight, and the red roof is a vivid reminder that safety and security are available.

For over a hundred years the Point Betsie light has been sending out its welcome glow to sailors and ship captains and fishermen on this part of Lake Michigan. Three coastguardsmen and their families live there, responsible for the various appointments that are part and parcel of their business, for weather reports and for the light itself. The light has evolved from a kerosene lantern moved by pulleys to a filament electric light. The fog horn has evolved from a throaty type, that just missed by a hair a full octave as it boomed "Bay-y----Rum," to an electronic moan at a single pitch that sounds off when the atmosphere reaches a certain density.

Exactly at the moment of sunrise the landlocked coastguardsman comes onto the lighthouse grounds to raise the flag. The cottage occupants with a slight degree of chauvinism do the same; and on any clear summer day there will be not one, but seven Old Glorys announcing the "flag is still there."

The lighthouse draws many people to it. The tourists come to show their children what a lighthouse is. They are often met with disappointment because they must only see it from afar. The men have sufficient work to do that they cannot give time to guiding sightseers, nor do they appreciate a constant invasion of privacy, the lighthouse being their home as well as their occupation. On an occasional weekend afternooon they do open the lighthouse to travelers, and there are always plenty of people waiting to see it.

The artists come to paint—setting up their easels in the sand, working with eyes squinted against the brightness of the sun. The structure is not really aesthetic in terms of design. It is more like a plump little woman than a willowy, tall beauty. But the beauty is there; and, in some ineffable manner, the drama and mystery of the light deserve to be captured for posterity.

Exactly one-half hour before sunset the light begins its nightly rounds, making a full circle that illuminates the lake and the dunes as it moves on its familiar course. Exactly one-half hour after sunrise the light goes off, and the work and polish begins again to have all in readiness at the next magic hour.

In the early years at Point Betsie I made a yearly

pilgrimage up to the light. The captain is very kind—
he sees me walking on the lighthouse path, and he
knows I'm not sight-seeing. I tell him why I have this
particular interest, so he takes me up the spiral metal
stair case that winds up through the light tower, up to
the top where the precious light is kept.

On my first visit I was astounded when I saw the
size of the light itself. The bulb is only one thousand
watts—hardly enough light to do the giant-sized job it
has to do. When I remarked about this, the captain
pointed out the set of reflectors surrounding the light.
The reflector system is one of the most aesthetic
things at the lighthouse. There are ten free-standing
prisms which completely encircle the small bulb. Each
prism is set into brass, which is kept highly polished,
so the shining prisms and rich brass become
themselves objects of beauty. These reflectors were
made in France and shipped to America in 1856. They
were installed in the Point Betsie light when it was
built in 1858. Because of them, the light is magnified
to 350,000 candlepower, visible on a clear night for
over fifteen miles.

The reflectors are nothing in themselves. They
could stand there as objects of beauty, but dead and
cold, for without the light there would be only
darkness.

At point Betsie, as darkness begins to settle over
the dunes and the lake, your eyes are naturally drawn
to the lake. The Christian is one who is willing to
stand exposed to the *lumen Christi,* the light of Christ.

The light from the Point Betsie tower sweeps over
the lake, searching out difficulty, a boat or a freighter
in danger. And the light of Christ searches out dif-

ficulties in our lives, illuminating us to become more self-aware.

It is a strong light, a brilliant light that can break through outer layers that seem impenetrable. It reaches deep into us where finally we come face to face with our own shortcomings, our own guilt. But when it reveals sin and guilt, the good in us comes into perspective too. Exposed to the light of Christ we learn to know ourselves; we become authentic persons.

As Douglas Steere says, "This kind of person knows sin for what it is, because he knows it within himself. Yet he is not overcome by sin for he knows the Light by which the darkness is revealed as darkness, and his trust is in that Light."

The light in the tower is Christ indeed. All the power, the strength, the way is in him. But we are the reflectors. We can, by living and believing in his light, reflect his nature to the world. Without our relation to Christ we are nothing. But knowing he reveals God's nature to us, knowing he walked the way of the cross, knowing compassion and love were his way of life, we can reflect in some slight measure his nature.

In the empirical church the power of Christ increases in direct ratio to those who reflect his nature. "He is in the world, and the world knows him not"— largely as Evelyn Underhill says, "because His members fail to disclose Him!" This is a poignant indictment against us. We do indeed "take the name of the Lord in vain" if we do not in our daily lives, in our limited spheres of influence, reflect the nature of Christ.

In Paul's letter to the church at Ephesus, he says to his followers, "For once you were darkness, but now you are light in the Lord; walk as children of light (for the fruit of light is found in all that is good and right and true)."

The total experience at Point Betsie sets us in the light, we reexamine life, we seek the fruit of light, that which is good and right and true.

The lighthouse looks indestructible, but the waves and the wind will take their toll. The *lumen Christi,* the light of Christ, will never be destroyed for "neither death, nor life, nor angels, nor principalities, nor things present, nor things to come, nor powers, nor height nor depth nor anything else in all creation, will be able to separate us from the love of God in Christ Jesus our Lord."

EPILOGUE

How many springs and summers and falls and winters have passed us by since that long ago spring when Point Betsie was our lodestar. We have gone back summer after summer, drawn there by things that seem unchanging. The cottages are still as they were— no new ones have been added. The dunes are the same, though we know the sands shift continuously; and the topography of the beach changes only slightly with the winds and the storms. The lighthouse remains invincible, unchanged.

In ways, our lives seem like that—and yet we are undergoing subtle changes constantly, both inwardly and outwardly. We are growing older and time takes its toll. The nest has emptied and we learn to deal with a silent house. Our two daughters have brought us two sons: Bunny's Patrick and Dawn's Raymond. And joy of joys, we have become grandparents to Hamilton Helman Hill, Bunny and Patrick's firstborn. This summer will be another Point Betsie "first" as all seven of us gather at the Cape Cod cottage and lovingly mix families and generations.

We have changed residences from 714 Bond to a large Tudor home in the hallowed college woods. The house, named Tall Oaks, is surrounded by the tall, sturdy, and ageless oaks from which it gets its name. Above the entrance of Tall Oaks there is a sign which says *Venit hospes, Venit Christus*—when a guest comes, Christ comes. The guests come in abundance, and we spread the table and celebrate the grace of God that flows between us.

As for me, I have come to a watershed time in my life. Our daughters are reared and have assumed responsibility for their own lives. I nurture from afar but they no longer need me in the vital physical sense they once did.

So I read and write and speak before many and varied groups. My hands say "use me," and I sculpt as another way of expressing those thoughts and feelings which reside in a deep and private part of me. I think of the sand dune we own at Point Betsie and visualize a permanent home there.

I continue in my quest for relationship—for union with God, and the gift of faith that lighted my way as a ten-year-old child comforts me daily. I am blessed with loving friends of the spirit, who attend me in satisfying conversations and who, in every way, help to make my prosaic life a constant and satisfying pilgrimage of love. I celebrate life daily in its humdrumness and its high moments, in its valleys and its peaks.

And almost daily some thoughts wander north to Michigan. I visualize the dunes and the lake and the lighthouse, and I ponder the great satisfaction that has come to us through a sense of place. Most satisfying of all is the fact that one of those sand dunes belongs to us—we are stewards of it for our lifetime, and the ownership assures us that we may always return to a place where we can quietly reflect on and recreate that interior life of the spirit that puts all of life into perspective.

My prayers are mostly prayers of gratefulness as I thank God without ceasing for work to do that demands a committed life, for a wide circle of family and friends and the spirit of love that attends these many relationships, and most of all for the "unspeakable gift which is Christ Jesus."